# Live
# FULL
# Die
# EMPTY

# Live FULL Die EMPTY

## Rick Godwin

**Bridge-Logos**
Gainesville, Florida 32614 USA

*Live Full—Die Empty*
by Rick Godwin
Copyright ©2004 by Bridge-Logos Publishers
All Rights Reserved
Printed in the United States of America
Library of Congress Catalog Card Number: Pending
International Standard Book Number: 0882709712


Scripture quotations from New King James Version, New Living Translation, and Amplified.


Published by:
**Bridge-Logos**
Gainesville, FL 32614
www.bridgelogos.com

# Dedication

I want to personally dedicate this book to everyone who has at any time in life felt overlooked, unwanted, or alone. God knows where you are, He loves you, and He chose you.

> *God says, "For I know the plans I have for you, they are plans for good and not for disaster, to give you a future and a hope."*
> —Jeremiah 29:11

# Acknowledgements

All men and women are compositions of experiences they've had, books they've read, people they've met, and places they've been. I'm certainly no different. Much of what I've learned in life I've learned from others.

I want to acknowledge some of those important people in my life. In my early days of ministry, I was privileged to have Casey Treat, Pastor of Christian Faith Center in Seattle, Washington, sow much into me regarding God's destiny for every human being on planet earth.

Charles Simpson was another mentor who taught often on the fact that God was purpose-driven. He taught this principle years before great people like Rick Warren had written anything on the purpose-driven church or purpose-driven life. Charles highlighted the fact that God uses people no one else would consider useable, and does extraordinary things with them.

What I know is that we never grow beyond the people around us. I've been privileged to have many great men and women influence me. I am a debtor to so many over the years.

My deepest gratitude to all!

# Table of Contents

# Living Full

God has put a lot more in you than you're living out. This might shock you, but your greatest fear should not be death. Your greatest fear should be that you die too soon, too easily, before God is finished with you. You don't want to die prematurely. That's when you haven't fully explored the purpose, potential and wonderful gifts that God created within you.

You want to live fully—your dreams fulfilled, your purpose triumphantly achieved, nothing left to give when you die.

You want to die empty. When you need a boost in your confidence, believe this: You don't have to die until you're finished.

Living full and dying empty isn't an art form; it's a decision. Most people simply exist without ever finding real life.

Television is filled with "Reality TV." Sadly, those watching these immensely popular programs never discover reality for themselves. You don't have to be an empty shell letting whatever fad or pop trend fill your existence with a momentary fix of excitement.

You're filled with potential that God wants to release in you right now. You can move from mere existence to overflowing, limitless life. But, you must decide.

**First**, decide to turn the pages and keep reading. Understand that this isn't just a book. It's a call to action. You must decide to dig deep within yourself to discover your potential and God's purpose. Then you must decide to move out from your negative past and into God's awesome future for you.

**Second**, you must decide to act on what you learn. Revelation without actions simply produces legalists who major in minors and focus on rules instead of relationships that make life productive.

Mired in the pit of complaints? Stop whining. It's time to move on or you'll exist forever in the wilderness of your own choosing.

**Third**, you must decide to put into action what you learn. It's your choice; you can live by design or by default. When you accept your present "fate" instead of following God's plan, you become a volunteer, no longer a victim.

Ready to move forward? Turn the pages. Make life-changing decisions. God is ready to walk with you into your potential so that you can *live full and die empty.*

Rick Godwin
San Antonio, Texas

Chapter

# —1—

# Live Full—Die Empty

It's a tragedy for any beloved child of God to die without realizing the gift of potential He has instilled in him or her. I urge you to respond to God's plan for your life. Listen to Him. Discover His vision for you. Live to your full potential, and when you die . . . die empty.

God paid a ransom to save you from the empty life you inherited from your ancestors. The ransom He paid was not silver or gold. It was the precious lifeblood of His Son, Jesus Christ—the sinless, spotless Lamb of God.

Demographic experts tell us that 5.8 billion people inhabit planet earth. Last night, another 124,000 were born. 124,000! All that human life exists on the planet; yet no two people are born with the same DNA or fingerprint. That means that God, with His awesome creativity, has produced in you an individual who can't be duplicated.

You're a unique specimen. There will never be another you. When you introduce yourself, exhuberantly proclaim, "Hello, meet an original!"

God isn't in the business of making carbon copies. He makes us each unique so that all humankind is a fascinating mix of diversity. Agreement requires diversity. Unity demands diversity. If all of us were the same, then life would be boring. Thank God, you're different from everyone else!

If two people are identical, then one is unnecessary. Why do you think God made you different from everyone else? He wants to teach you the principle of scarcity. Economists theorize that the value of something is determined by how rare it is; that is, the scarcer something is, the more it's worth.

Oil, diamonds and gold are valuable because they are beautiful . . . and scarce. At the other end of the value spectrum, we see the unattractive . . . and plentiful. For instance, an asphalt parking lot qualifies as the latter. Men have sold their souls to steal and horde oil, diamonds and gold. But I've never seen anyone jump out of his car, dig up a chunk of asphalt and dash home to hide his stolen plunder. Asphalt isn't a rare commodity.

## Don't Believe the Lies About You!

You're a rare commodity. God made you unique and irreplaceable. To appreciate God's gift, you must recognize how incredibly precious you are. The devil will try to devalue you through negative thoughts, anxiety, and demeaning words that break your spirit. If you succumb to the devil's lies, you will ultimately abandon relationships, responsibilities and, perhaps even life itself. Even worse, the enemy wants to convince you that you're worthless so that you will abandon God's will for your life.

If you believe the lies that you're worthless and have no value, you will lose hope and be blinded to God's purpose for your life. The devil knows that if you have no vision, you won't see a reason for living.

Shocking statistics tell us that suicide is the third leading cause of death among 15-to-23-year olds. According to the Center for Disease Control, suicide in the United States was responsible for 30,000 deaths last year. That exceeded the number of homicides! More people died by their own hands than by murder because they felt hopeless and valueless.

> Jesus did not die to make you valuable; He died to prove how valuable, how precious you are to Him.

Never forget how valuable you are. You're as valuable as the ransom God paid to purchase you back.

Jesus did not die to make you valuable; He died to prove how valuable, how precious you are to Him. Your personal price tag is amazing. You're worth the death of the Son of God. On your worst day, you are worth the death of Jesus.

What a valuable person you are! Never demean yourself. When you look in the mirror, say,

> *"I am a person of heavenly value.*
> *God did a good thing when He made me!"*

Believe the truth of God's Word. When He created humanity, He said, "Good." Ask God now to permanently destroy your doubts about how significant and valuable you are. When He created *you*, God said, "Good!"

## Don't Waste God's Gift—You!

Contrary to popular belief, the wealthiest places on planet earth are not the oil fields in the Middle East or the gold and diamond mines of South Africa. The wealthiest places on planet earth are cemeteries. Buried in cemeteries are books that will never be written, dreams that will never be fulfilled, and ideas that will never be spoken. Cemeteries are repositories for visions that never became realities and songs that have never been sung.

People take to their graves their dreams and their passions. Great businesses are forever lost; they will never be built. Ministries and churches have been swallowed up in the earth. People die with the awesome dreams God gave them stored in their hearts.

The awesome power of potential is buried.

In Matthew 10:8, Jesus mandates the Church to raise the dead, heal the sick, cleanse the lepers and cast out demons. A person can be as dead as a corpse in a cemetery even while his or her heart is beating. Spiritually dead people are emotionally dead. Their dreams have died along with their talents, gifts and hopes. We must not let that happen to us. We must overcome spiritual death and awaken all that God has put inside us.

God has put into your heart awesome potential because He has called you according to His purpose (Romans 8:28). Every week of every single month of every year, people are raised from the dead by the good news of Jesus Christ.

## You Are Potential!

The wealth buried in cemeteries is called Potential. Potential is untapped power. Dormant ability. Unused strength. Hidden power. Unused success. Undiscovered wealth. God is a God of potential, which means that His power is hidden. His power exists but it's hidden. If potential is never seen, then potential defines who you really are.

What does potential do?

- *Potential* speaks of what you can do, but haven't done yet.
- *Potential* indicates how far you can go, but haven't gone yet.
- *Potential* promises how much you can accomplish, but haven't accomplished yet.
- *Potential* doesn't refer to what you have already done.

What you have already done is no longer your potential. God isn't interested in your past accomplishments. He is a God of potential. Once you have realized some of your potential, He says, "Okay, now do something else." That's why God says in Hebrews 11:6, "So, you see, it is impossible to please God without faith" (NLT).

So, what God is saying is, "Without faith, you don't please me."

It doesn't take much faith to continue doing what we're already doing. So He challenges us to have the faith to do what hasn't been done, to take that extra step past our comfort zone and move to the next level. God says in Romans 14:23, ". . . for whatever is not from faith is sin" (NKJV). After we accomplish something, it's done, and it's time to move on to the next level of faith, to continue developing your potential.

The indictment on the church is that most people are sitting comfortably at some level of accomplishment, assuming that they are pleasing God, but I think God is saying, "Boring! Now what?"

Maybe you're living a lifestyle as a community leader, a husband, a wife, a business owner, or an employee, and you're completely comfortable because your life's routine doesn't require faith. You might be a church member who tithes and gives at a level that suits your comfort zone. You might feel that since God has proven Himself faithful and you're a good person, all is well. However, your faith isn't being exercised, and you're not growing. Then one day you suddenly find yourself in a challenge and taking a risk that makes the hair stand up on the back of your neck. So, you think to yourself, "God, if you don't come through for me, I'm sunk!"

When you step out in faith, trusting in God, He says, "That pleases me. I like you out there just on the edge—always growing, taking another step of faith. When you're living complacently in your comfort zone, you're sitting in the lap of your worst enemy—the devil himself."

## Overcome That Which Limits Your Potential

In Ephesians 3:20, Paul says, "Now unto Him who is able to do exceedingly, abundantly, above all you ask or think according to His mighty power that works in us" (NKJV). The power of the Almighty, Omnipotent God is in you by faith. Why, then, do you find yourself settling for a humdrum life if the power of God resides in you?

It's because you have allowed false limitations on life into your mind and mouth. If you can't fathom abundance in your life, you won't believe that God has the power to provide abundantly for you. Your small thinking will prevent the power of God from working in your life.

We, as Christians, think too small.

Wouldn't it be awesome if you were the first person in the entire world whom God rebuked and disciplined for being audacious in

> Wouldn't it be awesome if you were the first person in the entire world whom God rebuked and disciplined for being audacious in your requests to Him?

your requests to Him? Can you hear God saying, "Well, you presumptuous thing, you! You want too much; you believe for too much; you think too big. Who do you think you are?"

That won't happen. Read your Bible. Jesus' admonitions sounded more like this: "You little, shallow-minded, pitiful people. I am amazed that you don't have any faith. You don't have any boldness, and you won't ask of me great things." Some of you are making God angry, and it's not because of some deep, dark sin. It's because you don't believe in God's infinite capacity to bring about greatness into your life.

Never measure your life by other people's opinions about you. Life is to be performed before an audience of one. It doesn't matter whether or not people like you, cheer you or applaud you. Your focus should not be the attention and approval of others. Keep your eyes on Jesus. If He isn't applauding you, you're in trouble. He is the only one you were born to please. He is the only one who knows exactly what He put inside you and what you're really capable of doing. Keep moving and keep pressing on until He gets up and shouts, "Well done!"

## What Do You Fear?

Let me give you some background on the church that I pastor. We began in a little motel room, moved to a high school, and then leased a dilapidated discount building. We finally purchased new property and presently conduct our services in a debt-free facility we call our church home.

Every move frightened me.

Fear will usually rear its ugly head as you make changes in your life and work. Every step we took, we took by faith by continuing to believe that our mission had favor in God's sight, even when the financial picture looked bleak. Fear showed up and said, "God's not going to come through for you. Better throw in the towel. Give up. It's over." But God always came through. He led us to resources we couldn't have identified if left to our own wits. God led us every step of the way. At every crossroad, we thought, "WOW, God came through!"

Each time He seemed to be saying, "You haven't seen anything yet!"

As I said in the introduction to this book, I want to restate again: God has put a lot more in you than you're living out. You're filled with potential and purpose. This might shock you, but your greatest fear should not be death. Your greatest fear should be that you die too soon, too easily, before God is finished with you. You don't want to die prematurely—when you haven't fully explored the wonderful gifts that God created within you.

You want to live fully—your dreams fulfilled, your purpose triumphantly achieved, nothing left to give when you die.

You want to die empty. When you need a boost in your confidence, believe this: *You don't have to die until you're finished.*

## Normality Is Failure

Human tendency is to compete with each other instead of completing each individual's God-given assignment.

When you're satisfied with accomplishment, misery and boredom seep slowly in. To be satisfied with mediocrity and be buried with normality is failure. The shocking truth is God did not give life to you to become a product of normality and mediocrity. Most people have been subnormal for so long that when they become normal, people think that they're abnormal.

We have normal people with normal faces conversing in normal conversations, keeping normal company, living in normal houses, driving normal vehicles, eating normal food, and buried in normal graves with tombstones of normal records of normal legacies. Yuck! So what? You were born to be unique—not to fit in, but to stand up and stand out. Don't get excited about what is. Get excited about what can be. What is to come!

## God Is a God of Potential

God is omnipotent. *Omni* means, "all, always." *Potent* means, "power, might, strength and energy." Only one person is ever ascribed the attribute of omnipotence, and that is God. God is all-powerful, almighty, and always filled with power beyond human understanding. If God is always full of potential, all He has done isn't all He can do. Remember, potential is never what you've done; it's what you can do but haven't yet done.

God created the galaxies. The Hubble Spacecraft's telescope has revealed 60 billion galaxies and still counting. There are hundreds of millions of planets in each galaxy—birthed through God. When God was finished, I can imagine Him saying, "You haven't seen anything yet!"

God is omnipotent. What that means is: *If you need something He hasn't yet created, He has the potential to create it!* Isaiah 55:9 reads, "As the Heavens are higher than the earth, so are my ways higher than your ways and my thoughts higher than your thoughts." You find it difficult to comprehend God because He has powers you haven't seen yet.

In John 1:1-3 we read, "In the beginning was the Word, the Word was with God and the Word was God. The same was in the beginning with God. Without Him nothing was made." Since God created everything, where was it all before it was known? It was in God. So, there was a point in eternity when there wasn't anything except God. Before all things were, He said, "I Am."

Think about God before anything was, standing on nothing by the corner of nowhere. Try to imagine God with everything inside Him, before anything was. Do you understand that? If you met God on the corner of nowhere on the sea of nothing and shook hands with Him, you would be shaking hands with everything. The problem is, you couldn't recognize the infinite possibilities because all things would still be in the form of potential.

## Be Careful How You Treat Others

You never know with whom you're shaking hands. If you remember this, it will change the way you look at people. Do not disregard anybody anywhere. You don't know what potential lies within someone after a superficial assessment.

CNN interviewed General Tommy Franks, commander of America's military forces in Iraq. He was explaining an encounter with one of his former professors. This professor had once stated that Franks was not the "sharpest knife in the drawer."

Years later, when the professor heard that his erstwhile pupil had risen to the status of Commander and Four Star General, he said, "I can't believe you're the Commander of all the Allied forces in America."

Franks' reply was, "Yeah, isn't this a great country?"

That professor had canceled Franks. Be careful how you treat people; you don't know the potential in anyone.

## Operation: Salvage

The Bible is a book of potential: a story of God collecting human rubbish and waste. He qualifies as an expert in garbage collection. Every time humanity throws someone away, God intercepts. God says, "You're not garbage. You're valuable. You're precious. I know what I put inside of you."

> Calvary, where the death of Jesus was executed, was the greatest salvage operation of mankind.

Calvary, where Jesus was crucified, was the greatest salvage operation of mankind. Jesus died to save those who deserved death and damnation, those who were abominations to God. Jesus didn't die for you because He felt like doing a good deed. He died because of His investment in you. What He placed inside you was more important than His life.

God did not save you to insure your passport to heaven. You'll go to heaven, but that's not the issue. God's immediate purpose is to secure the potential and vision you were born to fulfill. That's why Christ was willing to die.

Why do you think God keeps you alive? Why does He heal you? Why does He prosper you? He doesn't want you in heaven right now. You were born to do something on this earth; you're impregnated with the treasure of God. You're carrying God's vision. When Jesus died, He said in essence, "I have finished the work you gave me to do, Father." On the cross, He cried, "It is finished."

Nobody took His life. Nobody intimidated Him. There were several attempts to take Him by force, several attempts on His life. He didn't worry or lose faith even in the most perilous of times and circumstances, because they could not end His life until His purpose was fulfilled.

The fact is: *you're going to die.*

Determine now, in your heart, that you will die on time—when you're empty. Don't die full of unused potential, and take to the grave the treasure God placed in you. Deliver the treasure so that when you die there won't be anything left.

Paul the Apostle endured formidable obstacles in his journey of faith—including at least seven imprisonments, several assassination attempts on his life and the pain and humiliation of being stoned by his enemies. At the end of his life, he said, "I have finished my course."

Essentially he was asking permission to die. Have you ever heard anyone say something like, "I don't know why

God has kept me around? We lost all the men in the unit and I was the only one saved. I don't know why God spared my life."

Here is the answer: *No matter how wretched you have been, no matter how unimportant you might feel, if you're still alive and breathing, there is something in you that God still wants you to do.*

Imagine for a moment that your doctor tells you that lab tests show cancer. Your immediate thought might be, "It's over." Instead, imagine that believe the report of the Lord that you're healed by His stripes (Isaiah 53). You have to change your way of thinking. The doctor's report is cancer, but the Word of God says, "By His stripes you were healed" "Is any one among you sick? He should call the elders of the church to pray over him and anoint him with oil in the name of the Lord. And the prayer offered in faith will make the sick person well. The Lord will raise him up.  If he has sinned, he will be forgiven" (James 5:14-15).  Fight back with God's Word. Say, "I'm not finished yet!"

> Let your life span indicator be determined by potential—not age, infirmity or heredity.

The enemy can throw obstacles in your path and it might look bad, but if your potential hasn't yet been fulfilled, you're not going anywhere! That's good news! Let your life span indicator be determined by potential—not age, infirmity or heredity. Those factors do not have the last say. God does.

## Show Up Before You Check Out.

***The key to dying empty is showing up in life.*** Many people become the aspirations of their parents, their culture or their denomination. They fulfill other people's expectations of them. Ask yourself:

- Who are you really?
- Do we really know you, or are you a reflection of your parents?
- Have we met the real you?

Upon discovering your true potential, you become a problem to society. You can no longer be manipulated. You can no longer be controlled. The "new you" has experienced a revelation: You know what God wants to do with you. That makes you a problem because you're no longer hindered by other people's opinions. Potential is dangerous because others can't always see it.

> Upon discovering your true potential, you become a problem to society. You can no longer be manipulated. You can no longer be controlled.

Who would have thought Moses, a guy living on Easy Street in an Egyptian palace, who became a murderer, would write the first five books of the Bible? What a loss to the world it would have been if God had not been able to see past Moses' reputation. But God did not let Moses' reputation prevent him from living out his potential.

God says His gifts and callings are irrevocable. You might mess up your life, but when you receive your gifts and calling, they don't cease to exist because you have veered off God's path for you. You can't invalidate them. When people saw Moses, they saw a killer and a fugitive. God saw a deliverer.

Maybe you have committed adultery, destroyed your life with drug abuse, ruined a career or abandoned your marriage. If you're breathing, be assured that God's promise is still in you. Give your messed-up life to God. Who would have seen in this killer Moses the Ten Commandments—the civic, moral and social laws of many nations? That potential was inside of a murderer.

## Cancellation by Classification.

Don't let labels limit you. What you do isn't who you are. What is in you? David was a king, a politician. He was also the greatest psalmist that ever lived.

God looked at a coward named Gideon and saw a mighty man of valor, a warrior who would save a nation. God sent an angel to him where he was hiding in fear. The angel said, "The Lord is with you, mighty man of valor" (Judges 6:12). Gideon must have said, "Who? Me?"

Jesus was a carpenter. Carpenter wasn't who He was; that was what He did. Jesus *is* the Son of God, the Savior of the world.

It's important to realize that God doesn't address you based on your history. He addresses you based on your future, your potential. He said to Jeremiah, "Before I formed you in the womb, I knew you before you were born. I set you apart. I appointed you as a prophet to the nations" (Jeremiah 1:5).

Rahab had a disreputable job that could be likened to a modern day lap dancer. But God saw her as a woman of potential, and entrusted to her the Messianic seed line. If you happen to be earning your living in a questionable career, hear this message: God isn't finished with you yet. He has great plans for you.

One of my dear friends is a respected neurologist. He comes from an African-American family that endured racial segregation and prejudice. Extremely poor, with no chance for a college education, he joined the United States Army and became an officer in order to fund his dream of going to medical school.

He told me of a first-time patient, an old, white redneck from the South, who took one look at the doctor and refused treatment because of his race. What a foolish man. He canceled expert medical attention, which was his loss. The doctor billed him anyway, and he still had to pay for the care that would have helped him. Be careful whom you cancel.

Here are the things you need to consider when seeking professional advice:

- Is this person qualified?
- Is this person smart?

NOT:

- What color is this person's skin?
- How many times has this person sinned today?

You should profile people on whether they are qualified or unqualified, intelligent or unintelligent. Qualification and intelligence are irrespective of race or creed. We want smart people who can get the job done. When you cancel people by classification, you rob yourself of a blessing.

In John 4:10, we read of a woman at a well who had five husbands. Paraphrasing this story, I would tell it like this. Jesus met this Samaritan woman and said, "Give me some water." She said, "Why do you, a Jew, ask me for water?" That is the same as saying, "Why do you a Lutheran, ask me, a Southern Baptist, for water? Why do you, a Charismatic, ask me, a Methodist? Why do you, a Hispanic, ask me, an African-American, for water?"

> "Cancellation by classification is an eternal, universal human failing."
> —Miles Monroe

Jesus said, "If you knew who I was . . ." The Samaritan woman had never met Jesus. She had no idea who He was. She had no idea of the potential in Him. Just because He was a Jew, she said, "You're a Jew; my kind has no dealings with Jews." In other words, "My pastor told me to stay away from people like you." My friend Myles Monroe often says, "Cancellation by classification is an eternal, universal human failing."

I know a number of successful young pastors who lead influential mega-churches and absolutely refuse to be labeled. They are true to their doctrinal beliefs, but they live bigger than a denominational nametag. They have learned that when we label ourselves, we limit our own capacity to have positive impact on others. We limit our potential. And when we label others, we diminish their potential as well.

**Potential is God's gift to you.** What you do with your potential is your gift to Him. D.L. Moody said, "If God is your partner, you can make your plans big." And the miraculous, amazing wonder of the gift of potential is that it is inexhaustible. But, you might protest, I'm seventy-five years old. Well then, you'd better get started!

Moses was 80 years old when he answered the call of God.

Caleb was well advanced in years when he discovered he was in the "wrong church." He spent 40 more years in the wilderness, in unbelief, running with the "wrong crowd."

Then, finally, he stood before Joshua and said the equivalent of, "I am as strong today as I was when I got into the wrong church—give me that mountain" (Joshua 15:11). That was his destiny. He lived to take that mountain. So can you.

## Amazing Keys to Your Potential

- You're a unique specimen. There will never be another you. When you introduce yourself, exhuberantly proclaim, "Hello, meet an original!"

- Jesus did not die to make you valuable. He died to prove how valuable, how precious you are to Him. Your personal price tag is amazing—you're worth the death of the Son of God. On your worst day, you are worth the death of Jesus.

- What a valuable person you are! Never demean yourself. When you look in the mirror, say,

  *"I am a person of heavenly value.*
  *God did a good thing when He made me!"*

- No matter how wretched you have been, no matter how unimportant you might feel—if you're still alive and breathing, there is something in you that God still wants you to do.

- Try to imagine God with all possibility inside Him, before anything was. . . .You couldn't recognize the infinite possibilities because all things would still be in the form of potential.

- Be careful how you treat people; you don't know the potential in anyone.

- The key to dying empty is showing up in life.

- Don't let labels limit you.

- When you cancel a person by classification, you rob yourself of a blessing.

# 2

# Discovering the
# Treasure In You

I want to walk with you as you look deep into your soul and see the powerful treasure God has placed there. You have been raised up with Christ to live a new life. Open yourself to Him that He might illuminate your heart. Once you discover the great blessings that dwell within you, you will know the calling that is your personal destiny, the treasure that is your very own; and your life will be enriched beyond all you ever could imagine.

God graces us with gifts so precious and so numerous that I am amazed how easily we overlook them.

Do you drown yourself in sorrow over what isn't, rather than celebrate what is? Let me assure you of God's promise that He has placed a great treasure in you. When you allow Him in, when you trust Him fully, He will illuminate your heart so that you might . . .

Discover the hope of His calling.
*You have a future.*

Discover the riches of His glorious inheritance in the saints.
*You have a treasure inside you.*

Discover the great power that is available to all believers.
*You're illuminated with the supernatural power of God's Holy Spirit.*

Hear what the Apostle Paul tells us in Ephesians 1:11-19 (NLT),

> *"Furthermore, because of Christ, we have received an inheritance from God, for He chose us from the beginning and all things happened just as He decided long ago. God's purpose was that we who were the first to trust in Christ should praise our glorious God. And now you also have heard the truth, the Good News that God saves you. And when you believed in Christ, He identified you as His own by giving you the Holy Spirit whom He promised long ago. The Spirit is God's guarantee that He will*

*give us everything He promised and that He has purchased us to be His own people. This is just one more reason for us to praise our glorious God.*

*"Ever since I first heard of your strong faith in the Lord Jesus, and your love for Christians everywhere, I have never stopped thanking God for you. I pray for you constantly, asking God, the glorious Father of our Lord Jesus Christ, to give you spiritual wisdom and understanding so that you might grow in your knowledge of God. I pray that your hearts will be flooded with light so that you can understand the wonderful future He has promised to those He called. I want you to realize what a rich and glorious inheritance He has given to His people. And I pray that you will begin to understand the incredible greatness of His power for us who believe Him."*

## Confession of Personal Discovery

*"I am a new person in Christ. My old life is dead and gone. I am raised up with Christ to live a new life. I have what God says I have. I am who God says I am. I can do what God says I can do. I am blessed in my spirit, soul and body. I am blessed in my family and relationships. I am blessed in my health and finances. Through Christ, I can overcome every problem. I can win in every circumstance. I am living my dream and fulfilling my destiny. My life is a success. I will do God's will on earth as it is in heaven."*

## You Have a Future

God has a calling for your life. What a privilege to receive a call from God. I've had a few impressive phone calls over the years from movie stars, athletes and political officials. I was with my friend, Ray McCauley, in Johannesburg, South Africa, when he received a phone call from then-President Nelson Mandela.

Calls from famous people can make us feel pretty important. Most of us don't receive phone calls from presidents and movie stars, but it doesn't matter, because such worldly calls pale when compared to a call from Almighty God. And we all have a call from God. It's the most important call we'll ever receive because it lays out our future.

> When the petty and painful circumstances of everyday life misguide you and you take your eyes off Jesus, the devil is lurking in the shadows to wreak mass destruction in your mind.

If you really knew what it means to be called by God, you wouldn't live the way you do. You would never feel like garbage, or let the devil dump on you and convince you, you're worth nothing. You would not allow darkness to loom in your soul. When the petty and painful circumstances of everyday life misguide you, and you take your eyes off Jesus, the devil is lurking in the shadows to wreak mass destruction in your mind.

How do you overcome darkness and the devil? *With God's Word.* Psalm 119:105 declares, "Your Word is a lamp to my feet and a light to my path." Flood your heart with light and joy in the revelation that God has called you. You have a future, and that's what gives your life meaning and purpose.

**Flood your heart with the light of God's Word, and expel darkness.** God has called you. You haven't been overlooked! We've all had our moments of doubt, fear and feeling left out like the little kid picked last on a team. The ugly duckling, the girl nobody asked out on a date. You don't have to understand everything that happens; you don't have to like everything that happens. But no matter how things are going in your life, have faith. Trust that God has called you.

It doesn't matter if the source of your misery is an ex-mate, a former boss or the devil himself. If you love God, you're called by His purpose, and He will redeem you from whatever is holding you captive. Romans 8:28 (NLT) promises, "We know that God causes everything to work together for good for those who love God and are called according to His purpose for them." So don't sweat it. Trust that God has a plan for your life.

In Jeremiah 29:11 (NLT), God says, "For I know the plans I have for you, They are plans for good and not for disaster, to give you a future and a hope." When Israel was caught up in idolatry, going into Babylonian captivity, away from God, into slavery, God's message for them in summary was simply this, *"I have a plan for you. I have a hope for you."* And God brought it to pass.

God can overrule anything happening in your life right now. He is all-powerful. It doesn't matter how trashed your life feels; you have a future and a hope. Never listen to the lie that God isn't working on your behalf.

At times it appears that God isn't looking out for you; you wonder if your file got put in the back of God's filing cabinet and He has forgotten you. You might be asking, *"God, Where are you?"*

> *"He won't let you stumble and fall; the one who watches over you won't sleep"* Psalm 121:3.

Know this: *your fears are unfounded. God is always there.* Psalm 121:3 promises, "He won't let you stumble and fall; the one who watches over you won't sleep." Your file isn't lost. Your future is in His hands.

My wife on several occasions has forced me, nearly at gunpoint, to attend a play. I can appreciate the theatre. The skill of the actors, writers, and directors can be awesome, but theatre doesn't have the lively pace and volume I look for in live entertainment. My idea of a good time is rocking out at an Eagle's concert.

God made each of us unique, and that's my idea of fun. You might disagree, but please stay with me. I'm trying to make a point. Although it might be torture for me to sit through a play, God shows me something even when I'm in a place I don't want to be. Here I am, feeling held captive, sitting in a darkened theatre with hundreds of people, and watching the action on stage. All of a sudden—blackout! Act one is over; transition is in effect.

In the blackout, you hear footsteps; you hear people moving props around. You can't see what they're doing, but you know they are setting the stage for act two. It's like those times when you feel as if nothing is happening in your life. But, if you listen carefully and give prayerful attention to God, you know that He is working—even during your life-intermissions. He never takes a break from your life. He is always setting the stage for the next exciting act.

**God can overrule any situation in your life.** Look at King David and what God did for him. He rose as a humble shepherd boy, rejected by his father and his brothers, and became a powerful King of Israel. The Bible says that he had a heart after God's own heart. But King David made terrible mistakes just as we do. Good men and women are capable of doing ungodly things.

David had an affair with Bathsheba. He should have been in battle with his men, but he felt bored one day and took a stroll outside onto his rooftop. He caught a breathtaking view of the scenery. Lo and behold, he saw a beautiful, bathing, naked woman! Holy cow! What's a man to do? David wanted her.

David knew that Bathsheba belonged to one of his loyal soldiers, but still he sent for her. They had intimate relations; she conceived. When they discovered that she was pregnant, they tried to conceal it. Failed attempts to cover the truth brought fear that her husband Uriah would find out, so David compounded his sin. He had Uriah murdered and tried to cover that as well.

Nearly a year later, the prophet Nathan came to David, and confronted him. David repented and accepted full responsibility for his actions. Deeply regretting the evil he had committed, he submitted to anything God asked of him.

Amazingly, David is listed in the genealogy seed line of Jesus Christ. When God compares good kings to bad kings in Israel, he compares them with David. He became the measurement of a good king. That is an absolutely amazing example of God's forgiveness!

> ————•◆•————
> . . . what boundless grace God gives you by blessing you with a future—despite your past.
> ————•◆•————

*Only God can bless a mess.* Only God can redeem a nasty situation. This doesn't give you license to make a mess, but if you do, what boundless grace God gives you by blessing you with a future—despite your past.

In the genealogy of Jesus it reads that David was the father of Solomon, and Solomon's mother was Bathsheba, the wife of Uriah, who was the guy that David murdered. God put Bathsheba in the seed line of the Messiah. The average church wouldn't have let her in. "Bathsheba, the adulteress," they would say. I doubt she'd be a keynote speaker at a women's Bible conference.

People would whisper, *Have you heard about her? She slept with the king, murdered her husband and then got married because she was pregnant!* Out of that mess, because of repentance, God brought forth Solomon.

Maybe you're in a filthy, pitiful mess right now. You're thinking there's no way out. You're convinced God can't bring anything good out of your situation. Whatever mess you're in today, give your life to God. His mercy and grace will triumph over the plan of your adversary, the devil. It's never too late to trust God. Remember what Paul says in Ephesians, "I pray that your heart will be flooded with light so you can understand the wonderful future He has promised to those He called. I want you to realize what a rich and glorious inheritance He has given to His people" (Ephesians 1:18 NLT).

## Confession of New Creation

*I am a new creation in Christ. I am a child of God. I am accepted into the Beloved. I am complete in Christ. I am free from the law of sin and death. I have the gifts of the Holy Spirit, and He resides within me. I am of a royal priesthood, a holy nation. I am God's chosen possession. I am more than a conqueror. I am God's workmanship, His craftsmanship. I am partner and partaker of God's divine nature. I am predestined according to His plan. I am the righteousness of God in Christ. I have been qualified to share in the inheritance of the saints. I am a joint heir with the Lord Jesus and all He achieved in His resurrection from the dead.*

## Treasure Is In You!

Paul writes, "I want you to realize what rich and glorious inheritance He [God] has given to His people" (Ephesians 1:18 NLT). He is speaking of hidden treasure. He is speaking of the treasure in you.

Years ago, I read about a bag lady discovered dead in her home. She lived in a rundown shack. When she died, investigators found trash bags filled with money, stocks and bonds worth millions of dollars. Her rundown life and her rundown shack were sitting on millions in unused wealth. Treasure, if it goes unused, isn't any good.

**You're a treasure.** You might not see it that way, but that's the way God sees it. Train your human spirit to see things the way God sees them.

How tragic that many Christians journey through life without a clue. Do you remember the hit sitcom, "The Beverly Hillbillies," during the 1960s? These song lyrics opened the show every week:

> *Listen to story about a man named Jeb, a poor mountaineer barely kept his family fed. Then one day, he was shooting up some food, and up from the ground come a bubbling crude. Oil that is, black gold, Texas tea. Well, the first thing you know, ole Jeb's a millionaire. Kinfolk said, "Jeb move away from there." Said, "California's the place you ought to be." So they loaded up the truck and they moved to Beverly . . . Hills, that is. Swimming pools, movie stars.*

Jeb is this rag-tag, worn down, broken-looking, old redneck man. He has holes in his shoes, torn up underwear and a rope holding up his trousers. Living without indoor plumbing, without running water, and in a state of absolute abject poverty, he was shooting squirrels for Granny to cook in the pot. I mean, it couldn't get any worse. And right under his feet are billions of dollars in oil. Shooting dinner one day, BAM! He hits an oil geyser and the rest is history. Ask yourself:

- Are you like Jeb Clampett?
- Are you sitting on top of untold riches while living life in a rundown shack?
- Are you oblivious to the fact that you've been set free from the power of sin?

You're a new creation in Christ, but you feel worthless. You have been given authority over the devil, yet remain oppressed because you're in darkness and you need your soul flooded with the light of God's Word. The devil is a lying, deceitful appraiser. He's a little like a used car salesman without a conscience. He tries to convince you the model car you want to trade isn't selling quite like it used to. The value has dropped and production has stopped. Soon, you feel like your car is a heap of junk. No wonder no one wants to give you anything for it.

Satan does the same thing when he devalues and undervalues you. He does it through your own thoughts and feelings, your blemished past, your failures and others' estimations of you. That personal devaluation comes from the evil one to beat you down and make you feel worthless. But, paraphrasing what Jesus says in John 8, "*Satan, listen, if your lips are moving, you're lying! You're a liar and the father of all lies!*"

> Personal devaluation comes from the evil one to beat you down and make you feel worthless.

Have you ever been on a long distance road trip listening to the radio? Sometimes, one station's signal weakens and another signal overtakes the station you're listening to. Keep traveling a few miles down the road and your original station returns beautifully in surround sound, as if never interrupted.

A good friend of mine said he was driving through the countryside listening to a message that said, "God loves you so much." He explained how rich the pastor's voice was—a really deep, great radio voice that sounded like God.

"God loves you so much," he began, when a high-powered 50,000-watt rock station overtook the pastor's message with the song, "You're no good, you're no good, you're no good, baby, you're no good."

My friend kept driving and the signal jumped back to the pastor's godlike voice restating, "God loves you so much."

The signal switched to, "I'm gonna say it again. You're no good, you're no good, you're no good, baby, you're no good." That is exactly what the devil tries to do to every one of us every day. We're tuned into God. He's saying, "I love you, you're valuable to me, you're so precious to me."

And the devil wants to bring interference, override our signal, and say, "No, no, no, you're nothing, you will never be anything of value." He's a liar!

On occasion, I've watched the Antique Road Show on television. People bring old junk that they've found or bought or inherited. They take it to an antiques expert to have it appraised. The expert might value their $5 object at $20,000! Fascinating. The owners leap frog across the screen, jumping for joy. Unbelievable!

One episode featured a gentleman who brought a painting he had purchased at a garage sale for 50 bucks. Its value was estimated at $3.5 million! He nearly had a heart attack. Wouldn't you love to have seen the reaction of the guy who sold the painting for 50 bucks? He must have had a heart attack! And to think, this sort of thing happens all of the time.

Esau, Jacob's brother, sold his birthright for a bowl of chili. Jacob did not steal it; he bought it. Somebody's been teaching Sunday school wrong. Esau sold out for a bowl of chili because he didn't place any value or privilege on the rights of a firstborn. Jacob saw the value and capitalized on it.

Satan benefits from you undervaluing the treasure in you. If you think you can't make it, you won't try. If you think God won't do it for you, you won't ask Him. Believe you're worthless, and you will never boldly, in faith, step out and do something for God.

*God's message to you is, "I love you; you're valuable."* Value is a strange thing. For instance, let's look at the value of a $20 bill. Go back in time to the day of its creation. Since that day, this $20 bill might have been abused, misused, unloved, and involved with criminal activity. Perhaps it was passed around like it was nothing, given up for sexual immorality, handed over for drugs, stolen for a lesser evil. It might never have been used for anything good. Yet, if I offered it to you, would you take it? Yes! Why? For the same reason I don't want to give it to you. The creator, The United States Treasury, determined its value at $20. All that it's been through did not determine the value of that bill.

In the same way, your personal value is worth as much to God today as the day you were born. Regardless of what you've been through. The value of your life is based on what your Maker says about you. Don't undervalue the treasure God put inside of you. Undervaluing the treasure neutralizes you. Flood your life with the Light of God's Word.

When I was in Johannesburg, South Africa, I visited the gold mines. I held in my hands a solid gold bar weighing 24 kilograms, 99.9 percent pure gold worth $1 million. It was tremendously dense and heavy. Did you know that to produce one single ounce of gold, miners must first remove tons of dirt? Wow! I had no idea.

> God will remove tons of dirt from you to reveal the treasure He placed in you.

A powerful truth resides here. When God develops us, it's a lot like gold mining. Gold miners don't look for dirt; they look for gold. God will remove tons of dirt from you to reveal the treasure He placed in you. All of us have dirt that needs removing. I've got good news for you. God is in the dirt removal business. He will forgive, cleanse, and change you by the power of the Holy Spirit within you.

## Confession of Personal Treasure

*There is a treasure in me. I have a future. I know the hope of my calling. The light of God's Word is flooding my life.*

## The Holy Spirit's Power Dwells in You!

The supernatural power of God's Holy Spirit is in you. This same power raised Jesus' dead body from the grave. In Ephesians 1:19-20 (NLT), Paul says, "I pray that you will begin to understand the incredible greatness of His power for those who believe in Him. This is the same mighty power that raised Christ from the dead and seated Him in the place of honor at God's right hand in the heavenly realms."

Paul is petitioning us as believers to wake up! The same power that raised Christ from the dead is in you right now. You've got it in you, on you, and around you. His presence, His Holy Spirit is with you right now. Most of us live life completely unaware of that. He gives you the power to do anything God calls you to do that you could not ordinarily accomplish on your own with your own resources.

Acts 10:38 (NLT) says, "And no doubt you know that God anointed Jesus of Nazareth with the Holy Spirit and with power. Then Jesus went around doing good and healing all who were oppressed by the devil, for God was with Him."

We need that power to encourage people, to give hope to those who are hopeless, and to transform lives. That power changes a human being who is apart from God and make him a believer in Christ so he can get a new heart and become a new creation. We need that power to remove sickness from a person's body, to break evil addictive forces. The Holy Spirit's primary purpose for empowerment is to help people.

You need power to change attitudes. I can remember hating my father. Growing up in a broken home, life with my father was tough. With his military background, "*Yes sir!*" was about the only phrase he wanted to hear from me. I didn't even have a first name until I was 18.

> "*What did you say, boy?*"
> "*Yes, sir!*"

Only God could change my heart and make me see him the way He did.

When light flooded my heart, I didn't excuse or obliterate the poor fathering or my father's bad behavior. I had a new power to change my response to my dad and adapt a new attitude. On my own, change would have been impossible. God's power can change you and give you a new heart, mind, and attitude. He can make you a whole new being. God can set you free.

God's power can change you . . . He can set you free.

If you're ready to go where the power is, pray, "Lord, show me how to help people."

Life should be dedicated to sharing God's blessing with others. How can you turn someone's life around and give him or her hope? How can we help people who feel as if life isn't worth living, find God's vision for them?

We need to realize that we have the power of the Holy Spirit to encourage them to get up and to recognize that life is just beginning. God anointed Jesus with the Holy Spirit and power, and He dedicated His life to helping others. That is what you should be doing. Ask God, "What can I do? How can I bless and enrich those around me?"

This isn't power that makes you glow in the dark. It's power that helps you touch people's lives and meet needs and change situations. You're an agent on assignment on this earth. You're God's representative, carrying His power.

Wake up! Live as though you have it! You're accepted, beloved; you have a great future. You have a great treasure in you and the power to do anything God calls you to do. Stop acting like an unwanted orphan. You have been adopted!

## Amazing Keys to Your Potential

- You have a future.

- You have a treasure within you.

- You're illuminated with the supernatural power of God's Holy Spirit.

- God's message to you is, "I love you; you're valuable."

- The Holy Spirit's power is within you, and gives you the power to change.

# —3—

# Overlooking the Extraordinary Potential of the Ordinary

God has a word for you that will change your life. But first you must wait, and listen, and be prepared to say Yes! when He calls. You must learn to see the extraordinary in the ordinary, as God sees the extraordinary in us. He knows where you are and where you're going, and He has the word that will set you free from your ordinary life. His word will open the door to the glorious, wondrous, and extraordinary potential that is your pre-destined future.

## A Nowhere Place Called Nazareth

To call Nazareth a town would be generous. By today's standards, it would be like a mobile home community that sprang up around a truck stop and came to life so truckers could bypass the valley and shave a few hours off their routes. No one would want to live there. No one would move there if they had a choice. The people who did live there were either born there or forced to stop off there because of economic woes. Or maybe they were running from the law.

The reputation of this horrible place was notorious. People said, "Nothing good here and nothing good comes from here." To complicate matters, the residents belonged to an ethnic group that was aggressively persecuted by the dominant culture surrounding them. You would think, having tasted the humiliation and sting of discrimination, they, of all people, would have been the least likely to dish it out.

But oddly enough, within their own social fabric, they practiced the same kind of discrimination they had suffered. And since the residents of this little village shared the same ethnicity, their discrimination targeted the poorest among them.

Here, if you were a man, and you had wealth or power or influence, you were at the top of the food chain. As you moved toward the bottom, you found poor females to be the lowest social class. The poor teenage girls who lived here were the least likely to succeed. One particular young girl was sort of pretty in an ordinary kind of way. If she had been a candidate for a makeover, she would have been dazzling. But the chance of such luxury coming her way was non-existent. Her destiny seemed pretty well set. She would probably get married, have a few kids and live her life barefoot, penniless, powerless and future-less.

Then something dramatic happened. Something extraordinary. God, for reasons we can't comprehend, was drawn to this poor, ordinary girl. How amazing that God would take notice of this girl whom no one had ever noticed before. For God to have notice her and been moved in His great heart toward her must have astounded all the angels in heaven.

God loved this little nobody girl living in this nowhere place with no chance for a real life, and He came to her and spoke. He offered this girl an incredible chance to escape her boring, dead-end life. His offer was genuine, and she was able to choose to accept or decline. God wouldn't have forced the offer. She thought about it for a moment and then, almost without hesitation, she responded, *Yes!* In doing so, she stepped into the will of God and walked onto the stage of history.

We know her as Mary, the mother of the Son of God, our Lord Jesus Christ. And as a 14-year-old girl in an impoverished nowhere place called Nazareth, the archangel of heaven, Gabriel, was sent to this poor girl with these words, "You are favored of God and He has chosen you to be the mother of His Son."

And Mary's response was, "Be it unto me according to your word." And the rest is history. God touched Mary, and she began to sing. She sang one of the most glorious poems that we have in world literature. It is called the *Magnificat.* "My soul proclaims the greatness of the Lord," she sang (Luke 1:46).

How does an illiterate fourteen-year-old girl with limited education and no tutoring in voice and music suddenly erupt with a soulful hymn that has since been chanted, prayed and sung by great voices for centuries? The answer is simple: God touched her.

> When you accept God's offer, you step into the will of God and onto the stage of history.

That same miraculous thing happens when God touches you. There are songs to be sung, books to be written, children to be brought forth, businesses to be started, careers to blossom, ministries to launch that can only happen when God touches you. And you will only feel His touch when you say, "Be it unto me according to your word." Or in a word, "Yes!" When you accept God's offer, you step into the will of God and onto the stage of history.

## Say "YES!" to God

Today we are blessed with the knowledge of history—we know, looking back, that this incredible event isn't just about Mary. It's about you and me. It's *my* Nazareth, *my* nowhere place. It's suddenly *my* nowhere life. It's *my* no-account being. Can any good thing come from my life?

And the answer in God is always *Yes!* But there are some conditions, some terms. God must come and make His offer. And I must respond, "Yes!"

But what will happen if you say "No!" to God? You alone have to think that through. What would your life be like from this point forward if you said "No" to God? Can you come up with an alternative better than God's? Are you that wise?

You couldn't love yourself more than God loves you. You could not possibly have a better plan for yourself than He has. He is omniscient—all-knowing. He is omnipotent, almighty, and all-powerful. He is omnipresent—everywhere at once. And you and I are way, way back in second place in that race. So prudence begs us to say "Yes!" even without fully understanding.

> The fact is, none of us can possibly know better than God, and we would be foolish to think we do.

The fact is, none of us can possibly know better than God and we would be foolish to think we do.

So from Mary, we learned that "Yes!" is the response God is always after, and in Mary's story, we learned three lessons of life. Here they are, simple and profound.

### Lesson #1:  Never overlook the extraordinary potential of the ordinary.

We live in America, in a culture that bombards us with the idea that we must own the latest, biggest and best. Everything is scaled up to epic proportions. Our entire worldview is continually assaulted with bigger, better, greater, thinner, shinier, brighter, faster, richer, and more powerful. It's tough to resist getting caught by the lure. We want the bigger big thing, the higher high, the faster fast, the prettier pretty, the weirder weird. And just when we've outdone ourselves, someone outdoes us. We stay driven toward the ultimate bigger, better or faster; and we miss the extraordinary potential in the ordinary.

Mary was just a peasant girl. What could possibly come from her? Outwardly, we don't see anything. But looking through God's eyes, we see a defining moment in human history. Never overlook the potential in the ordinary.

Your life today might be ordinary, nondescript. You might appear to simply blend into the status quo of life. Maybe that youthful passion that used to challenge you and make you dream of great things is giving way to slow surrender. Maybe you're passively agreeing to live a bland life in a joyless succession of meaningless days.

My suggestion is, "Don't do it." Don't overlook the incredible potential in the ordinary. Because what you find is that God touches ordinary people at special moments in history. What you find is that God comes to people with ordinary IQs, working at ordinary jobs and living in ordinary places, and does extraordinary things. But we always want to run to the next extraordinary place thinking, *"Maybe somebody will discover me there. Maybe I'll find what I seek in the business world, or the media world, or the entertainment world or the ministry world."*

> What you find is that God comes to people with ordinary IQs, working at ordinary jobs and living in ordinary places, and does extraordinary things.

And so, what could possibly happen that would incredibly impact our lives, our destiny, our nation, and our culture in an ordinary place? That is the whole beauty of this story.

Don't overlook, like most do, the extraordinary potential of the ordinary with God. That ought to give hope to every ordinary person. And I am one of the ordinary, and perhaps you're one of the ordinary.

Don't give up that passion and that dream. If you think you have no hope, it is an enemy plot from the devil himself, whispering to you, "Give it up, loser."

Ignore the enemy's whispers. God is drawing near, speaking to you with an offer. He will touch you as He touched Mary. He will usher forth from you a life that is glorious, holy, wonderful, and powerful—a life to be lived for His honor and His glory. But you have to want His offer. You must be willing to discover the extraordinary potential in the ordinary. Never count God out.

One of the most important things we can tell our kids . . . and I can tell believers is this: *"If you're faithful, if you pray and listen to God, then what He speaks to you will come to pass right where you are. God will come to you where you are."*

> If you're faithful, if you pray and listen to God, then what He speaks to you will come to pass right where you are.

Why do we panic about life and wring our hands? Because we don't trust God. We believe our jobs are too ordinary. Our marriages are too ordinary. But ordinary isn't bad. Remember the story of the fishes and loaves? In John 6:8, we are told about a small, ordinary boy who comes to Jesus with five loaves and two fish—by our standards, a Happy Meal. He presents his bounty to Jesus as Jesus' disciples are wondering how to feed 5,000 people.

Five loaves and two fish couldn't make a dent in the hunger of this mighty crowd. Andrew, Jesus' disciple, echoes our own skepticism when he says, "Well, what is that?" Andrew was a lot like we are. *"What is that?"* We ask such a question unable to see beyond the small, the ordinary. *"What is that? How is that going to feed 5,000 people?"* Andrew doesn't see anything extraordinary. He sees five loaves and two fish. But the boy gives it to Jesus and the miracle begins. Jesus takes that little Happy Meal and feeds 5,000 people and after the meal, he gathers up the leftovers—12 baskets full. Never overlook the potential of the ordinary.

It's okay to brag if it's true and it's about Jesus. I remember when the church that I pastor didn't have anything. We weren't considered to be anything out of the ordinary. We hadn't accomplished anything noteworthy. Most people saw us as an ordinary church. But now, years later, we are emerging on the stage of church history in mega proportions and people who did not notice us before are wondering, *Where did you come from?*

We were right under their noses, but they didn't see us because they thought we were ordinary and our mission was ordinary. We didn't have gold dust on our faces but we were here and faithful and strong and listening to God. As a result, God has brought something extraordinary out of a group of ordinary people. I know it. I have always known it. I have watched it. I am absolutely convinced of the extraordinariness of our faith, our work and our walk with Jesus.

I am certain that Jesus can take your ordinary ability, your ordinary life, your ordinary marriage and your ordinary heart, and in one touch, infuse them with extraordinary potential. A mother might say of her ordinary child, "Honey, we will have to help him through life." Nah. God will touch that child one time and everything will change. And that's what the faithful have that the secular world doesn't have: *With God's help, we can find extraordinary potential in the ordinary.*

> I am certain that Jesus can take your ordinary ability, your ordinary life, your ordinary marriage and your ordinary heart, and in one touch, infuse them with extraordinary potential.

### Lesson #2: Never underestimate the power of a personal word from God to you.

Let's imagine the conversation between Mary and Gabriel as having gone something like this. The angel Gabriel said, *"Hail, Mary."* It was a greeting like, *"Hi, Bob. Hello! Shalom. Hail, Mary!"* It was a greeting—not a sacred religious expression. It was an angel in person trying to make a friendly impression so he wouldn't scare this poor little mortal half to death. *"Hey, I'm Gabriel. Please don't freak out. I am sent from God. Hail, Mary! You're a favorite of God and highly blessed for He has chosen you. I don't know why!"* Angels don't know why. They do as they are told. They are better than most of us: they are obedient to God. Can you imagine how Mary felt? This must have been the dream of every Jewish girl—to be the mother of the Savior of the world.

Remember what God told Satan in Genesis 3:14, in the presence of Adam and Eve after their fall into sin? He said, and I paraphrase, *"I will put an everlasting war between you, Satan, and the woman's child. This war will go on and on. There will be times you seem to prevail and triumph. But every success you have will be nothing more than bruising his heel. His triumph, however, will be the crushing of your head."* He was speaking, of course, of the Messiah who would be born of the woman. God made that promise. And in His promise, He gave hope to Adam and Eve even though they had caused the fall of mankind.

And that hope of the coming Messiah child was passed from generation to generation so that every Jewish woman wanted a male child more than life itself —with each birth, Jewish mothers whispered, *"Could this be the Messiah?"* There were a few who looked promising— Moses, Samuel, John the Baptist. But each of these heroes from the Bible was absolutely clear in declaring, *"I am not the One."* Mary was aware of that hope too, and in her heart, she probably wondered, *"Could I be the mother of the Son of God? Nah, there is probably a prettier girl who lives in Jerusalem a few blocks from the Temple."*

It's always that way. We always think the good stuff is happening to somebody else, somewhere else, don't we? Always. We muse, *"Well, if I lived there, and if I had that and if I were married to him and if I had that job, and if I could just geographically move."* But all you need is a word from God: it doesn't matter where you live, what you have, to whom you're married or where you work.

And so Mary had no real idea she would be chosen. Little did she know she was marked to be the mother of Jesus. But the Lord chose Mary, and Mary asked, "*How can this be? I'm not even married!*" The angel told her that the Holy Spirit would overshadow her and that she would bear a child and He would be called the Son of God. God spoke it. And it happened.

God spoke to a 100-year-old man named Abraham and a 90-year-old woman named Sarah, and said, "*You're going to have a baby.*" You understand that this wasn't a couple who were likely to conceive. Circumstances said they wouldn't. Biological reality said they couldn't. But God's words are life—powerful and creative. He spoke words and created the world. He created something out of nothing.

When God speaks a word to you, you will feel His life, energy and power. And that 90-year-old woman gave birth on a word from God. I tell you what—all you need is one word from God. You don't have to hear 42 sermons or read 142 books. Just one word.

> And when God speaks a word to you, you will feel His life, energy and power.

When God speaks, you can be saved. You can be changed. You can be called. You can open your mind to new possibilities when God speaks to you. You can discover that you can now do things that once seemed beyond your reach. You just need a word from God: *a living word.* Because God's word has power that impregnates your soul, His word makes the improbable, the impossible come to pass.

Ecclesiastes 8:4 declares, "Where the word of a king is, there is power." When Christ, our King, speaks, it's a done deal. Never underestimate the power of a personal word from God to you. Does your heart feel touched right now? Is He speaking to you right now?

You will know because one word from God is more meaningful than a thousand words from a mere mortal. In your heart, God is speaking to you. He is bringing up things. He is stirring up old dreams that you have allowed to slumber. He is rekindling fire that has almost gone out. God is drawing near to you. Are you listening?

Never, never, never underestimate the power of a personal word from God to you. If He speaks it, it's done. All you must do is say, "*Yes!*"

### Lesson #3: Never hesitate to say Yes! to any offer God makes you.

Never hesitate to say, "Yes!" to God's will for your life. Hear these words from Ephesians 2:10 in the Amplified Bible, "For we are God's own handiwork, His workmanship, recreated in Christ Jesus, born anew that we might do those good works which God predestined, planned beforehand, for us taking paths which He prepared ahead of time."

When you hear people say, "You make a way where there is no way." It sounds good, seems good, and makes for effective preaching, but it isn't true because He has already prepared a way. He prepared it before I got here. My job is to find it, get on it and move on it. That's it. He has already predestined my path. He's not *making a way where there is no way.* The *way* is out there. I've just got to get on it.

You might say, "Oh, but I need to create my own world." No, you don't. He has already created it. Do you write your own future? No, you just discover it. You discover it when you yield, when you say, "Lord, what you say, I will do. Where you lead, I will go."

Some folks think God isn't speaking to them unless some blatant charismatic occurrence zaps them. They're waiting to be sprinkled with gold dust or pigeon feathers, or for oil to appear on their hands. Come on! Get real! Wake up! There is just one thing that needs to happen.

You need to say to the Lord, "Lord, if you tell me, if I know you tell me, I will do it." You must say and believe, "I will get the will of God. If you will show me, I will do it. Yes, sir! That is the only good thing I've got going in my life. I will do it. It might take me awhile to see it. Pray for me. But if I see it and hear it, I will do it."

And I'm telling you, that is the secret to success. It is the only thing you need. Because God has promised He will bring it to you. You don't hunt it. He brings it to you.

And I say to anybody, when He opens the door, go through it. Wait for Him to come to you, and He will come. Meanwhile, be faithful right where you are.

God knew He was going to bring David to the stage of history. David wasn't passing out resumes and looking for a job. David was playing a guitar and keeping the flock. And on an ordinary day, this ordinary boy took some ordinary chickens to his brothers, and destiny knocked in the form of a giant. Did God set him up? Yes. But it was on an ordinary day in an ordinary place.

Don't be impatient. If nothing seems to be happening, you might need to chill. The problem isn't with the Lord. The problem might be with you. Invite Him into your heart, and then be patient and wait—and in the waiting, be joyous with the ordinary, and the extraordinary will come out of it. And when He makes an offer, just say, "Yes!" He says we should walk the path He has prepared ahead of time. We are living the good life that He has prearranged for us. What kind of life do you have? The good life. That's the promise of the Lord (John 10:10).

Some of you think the will of God requires that you marry some old ugly mate and endure an impoverished life in a tent in a third world country, doing God's work. You're wrong, unless that is a passion in your heart. He won't do that to you. He made you. He has a stake in you. He is your parent, and He wants you to live a life that brings joy to you so that you can bring joy to others.

I think our fear is that of the unknown. What is He going to do? Where is He going to send me? How bad is it going to be? Well, think about what you've done to your life in trying to arrange everything yourself. It couldn't get worse. It will, in fact, get better. In Jeremiah 29:11 (NIV), God says, "I know the plans I have for you . . . plans to prosper you and not harm you, plans to give you hope and a future." God has chosen a path for your life, and no employer, no lull in the economy, and no pink slip can stop it.

If you have ever said to yourself, *"I think I can come up with a better idea than God,"* then let me tell you, you're wrong. There is no better idea than what God has for you. Psalms 47:4 promises, "He shall choose our inheritance for us and his choice is excellent." Say, "Lord, I don't want to choose. I trust you to make the perfect choice for me."

Psalms 16:6 reads, "The lines have fallen to me in pleasant places." Here's the same verse in New Living Translation: *The land you have given me is a pleasant land.*

What a wonderful inheritance! What God has in mind for you isn't a bad deal. When you let the Lord choose your inheritance, you're embarrassed because you and I would never have chosen that much abundance. But never hesitate to say, "*Yes!*" to God. What could possibly be working in your brain to say *No*? God wants to take my disease and give me healing. He wants to give me joy for sorrow. He wants to take my frustration and give me fulfillment.

So never hesitate to say, "Yes!" to God's will for your life. That's exactly what Mary did. And God is reaching down in your Nazareth life right now. Has any good thing ever come out of Nazareth? Maybe that's what you've said about yourself or your situation. But in that average, ordinary life of no hope, no future and no real success, God comes and speaks.

Your Yes! plus God's Yes! equals Yahoo!
—Dave Owen

If your life feels ordinary, if your circumstances seem hopeless and dull, do not succumb to the venomous voice of the devil. Look beyond the ordinary and see the extraordinary that lies within.

Why lament what isn't, when you could be celebrating what is to come? Savor the everyday blessings in your life, and prepare to receive the word. God has a word for you. He will come to you with bountiful blessings and the promise of a wondrous future—and all you have to do is say, "*Yes!*"

## Amazing Keys to Your Potential

- Never overlook the extraordinary potential of the ordinary.

- If you're faithful, if you pray and listen to God, then what He speaks to you will come to pass right where you are.

- Never underestimate the power of a personal word from God to you.

- When God speaks a word to you, you'll feel His life, energy and power.

- Never hesitate to say, "Yes!" to any offer God makes you.

- God has already made a way for you. It's your job to say, "Where You lead, I will follow."

# —4—

# Seven Keys to Discovering Your Purpose

How different would your life be if you stopped what you're doing today, listened to God, discovered His plan for your life, and dedicated yourself to living out that plan? I pray with you that these seven keys will help you unveil God's promise for you . . . that you might discover your gifts and be profoundly blessed.

When you discover God's purpose for you, you will be blessed with a sense of deep fulfillment. Nothing else in your life could be more important.

Have you ever asked yourself why God made you? What was His purpose, His destiny for your life? I challenge you to seek the answer, and once you know, you must accept that destiny, embrace that purpose and dedicate your life to fulfilling it.

I believe many people fear that if they submit their lives to God, He will make them do something they don't want to do. Dismiss those fears because they are unfounded. God would never call you to do anything that He hasn't already equipped and purposed you to do.

In Philippians 3:12, Paul says, "I don't mean to say that I have already achieved these things, or that I have already reached perfection. But I keep working towards that day when I will finally be all that Christ Jesus has saved me for and wants me to be" (NLT). His struggle isn't about getting to heaven; it is about discovering why God made him and why God apprehended and saved him. Once he knew that, he was able to fulfill his purpose and destiny.

These seven keys to discovering your purpose and calling are keys that are built into you by design, nature, gifting and ability. God always provides for His purpose. As you read this chapter, I encourage you to find the thing God made you to do—the thing that makes you come alive when you're doing it. I want you live a dream, a passion, a destiny. Give yourself to God with all of your heart, glorify Him with your life and when you do, you'll feel His pleasure.

**Key #1: God's purpose for you preceded His creation of you.**

Before He made you, God designed a purpose for you. Jeremiah 1:4-5 reads, "The Lord gave me a message. He said, 'I knew you before I formed you in your mother's womb. Before you were born, I set you apart. I appointed you as my spokesman to the world.'"(NLT)

You have a God-ordained purpose hard-wired into your mainframe by the Creator. It doesn't matter how, when or where you arrived. Did your parents want a girl and you were a boy? Were you conceived in the back seat of a Ford by two hot-blooded people engaging in illegitimate sex and who couldn't make a commitment to marriage? Were you an orphan, an outsider, a victim of abuse? Or perhaps you had the good fortune to grow up in a loving, supportive family?

Whatever your circumstances at birth, whatever your childhood story, whatever your life in the intervening years, all that matters now is this: *You can be awakened and encouraged to know that God had a purpose for your life even before you got here.* All you have to do is give your life to the God who manufactured you so you can fulfill that incredible, predetermined purpose!

You're not a misfit. You're not a mistake. You're important to God and when you understand His purpose for you, your life will truly have meaning. If you haven't entered into a personal relationship with Christ, do so now. A simple prayer of faith can begin your covenant with God. Pray this, "God, thanks for showing me your love through Jesus. I receive Jesus Christ as my personal Lord and Savior. I repent of my sins and surrender totally to Jesus' purpose and good plans for my life. Amen."

## Key #2: Your purpose determines your design.

Every engineer knows that function or purpose dictates the design process. Think about some of the most astounding engineering feats of our lifetime.

Have you ever seen a stealth fighter? Its fascinating, strange appearance differentiates it from any other aircraft. Composed of right angles, triangular shapes, low silhouettes, and black radar-absorbing paint, it's designed to achieve its purpose: avoiding radar detection.

When British Air and Air France teamed up to build the Concorde—the world's first supersonic airliner, its purpose was determined before its design. Before it was retired, I had the pleasure of flying on that airplane twice—three hours, 15 minutes from New York to London. 60,000 feet, 1,435 miles per hour, twice the speed of sound at 25 miles per minute! No highway patrol can catch those guys. We don't have a jet fighter in our inventory that can stay with the Concorde for more than three minutes. It is a phenomenal aircraft—sleek and slender, with a six-pack on each of its thin wings. You can't carry your mother-in-law and fourteen bags on this plane because it was built small and narrow to soar high and fast. Its purpose determined its design.

> God is the greatest engineer and He designed you.

Now, the brilliant engineers who designed the stealth fighter and the Concorde do not have a fraction of the power of The Greatest Engineer of All—God. He designed you. Your design is perfect for His purpose.

Stop arguing with the mirror. Stop arguing with others' expectations of you. You're unique, different and purposed for God. Every item you use each day, from a common teaspoon to stir your coffee to a cutting edge computer system to conduct your business, has a unique function, and so do you. God designed you for His purpose.

Everything and everyone has a purpose. Consider the many different types of churches. Each is designed to reach a certain population. At the church I pastor, we offer hour-long express services tailored to reach a generation on the go. The music, the message and the environment are conceived to meet the needs and lifestyle of this generation. Because our purpose is to reach a particular group, we design the service and the church to accomplish that purpose.

A different group might feel at home in a 100-year-old traditional church where the music comes from a hymnal, and the worship service is common to the denomination to which the church belongs. It would be altogether different, but it would have a purpose, just as our church has a purpose. Purpose determines design.

So do not argue with the designer who created you, and ask, "Why did you make me this way?" His design is perfect for His purpose. God did not make you wrong. He did not look at you and say, "OOPS, messed that one up!" There's nothing wrong with you! God made you just right. He gave you the right plumbing and the right chemistry because He doesn't make mistakes.

Your mistake is listening to somebody else tell you that you're not quite right. The manufacturer is the only one who can tell you why something was made and how it should be used to get the maximum effect. God is your manufacturer. He made you, and it is He who has the plan and purpose for you. The only one who wants to corrupt God's purpose for you is the enemy, that skulking devil who shields his evil motives under many guises.

Do not listen to the devil. Pay no attention to the voice of doubt. It is the devil whispering, trying to throw you off track. Accept yourself as God made you. He doesn't make defective products!

## Key #3: Your purpose predicts your potential.

It isn't the other way around. Potential doesn't predict your purpose. It's your purpose that determines how much potential you have. Have you ever heard the phrase, *"Oh she is so full of potential?"* This phrase is particularly popular among teachers who are trying to spare your feelings and those of your child. It might be painfully obvious to you that your child isn't gifted as an athlete or artist or ballerina. But some teachers are motivated by money and keeping their dreams alive. So, to keep your child in their program, they will say, with crossed fingers and forked tongue, *"She has potential."*

Let's face it . . . the idea of potential is overrated. Someone who has a gift will catch on quickly and keep improving with practice. I know a lot of Christians, loaded with potential, who never do anything for the Kingdom of God. Lots of things have potential. A package of new batteries is loaded with potential, full of power. But those batteries will never accomplish anything until they're plugged into their purpose. You have to hook them up to a CD, a flashlight, or a radio. The purpose for which they were made will then determine their potential. Potential by itself is worthless. Just like those batteries, you have to plug your life into the purpose for which you were created.

Paraphrasing Paul in Philippians 3:12, *"I press to know that purpose."* You have to know and press to find out what you're designed to do. Proverbs 26:13 reads, "The slothful man says there is a lion in the street and he won't go to work." There aren't any lions in the street. Get your lazy behind off the couch. The whole issue is an excuse for not going to work. As long as you make excuses, you'll never walk into God's purpose. Excuses are the crutches of the uncommitted.

Some people blame their inadequacies on a lack of discipline. I say they have a lack of vision. Discipline is never the objective. Discipline is a byproduct of a vision, of a destiny. When you want to achieve something, you must be willing to pay the price to get it. You might say, "I want to make more money. I want to be more effective in my witness. I want to build a more effective church." Your goal, vision, and destiny will produce a discipline in you that enables you to achieve it. Once you see it, you can keep moving toward it.

> When you want to achieve something, you must be willing to pay the price to get it. "Unto whom much is given— much will be required" (Luke 12:48).

God says that where there is no vision, people cast aside their strength because they have no discipline. Why? Because discipline comes out of a vision. Don't waste time beating yourself and others up by thinking you need more discipline. What you need is more *vision*, a clearer vision of God's purpose for your life.

The same principle applies to our children. Discipline by itself doesn't come out of a destiny; discipline alone results in legalism and bondage. Putting out a bunch of rules and regulations doesn't help anyone. You, as a parent, must instill vision in your children, and help them understand the reasons that vision is essential to their lives. Believe in your vision for yourself. Make your argument convincing, and your children will be willing to pay the price to achieve their vision. They will learn self-discipline when they're motivated by vision.

Vision is also necessary for Christians to be disciplined in their work and their faith. For years, churches have preached rules and regulations without vision and without purpose. Pointless regulations and meaningless discipline lead nowhere. Discipline comes from vision. With vision and discipline, you'll discover your true, God-given potential.

### Key #4: God's purpose is nestled neatly in your nature.

Webster defines nature as the particular combination of qualities belonging to a person by birth, origin or construction. God's purpose is nestled in you and comes naturally out of you. When I say God's purpose is nestled in your nature, I mean that it is what you do naturally. Birds are not only designed to fly; they love to fly. Fish love to swim. Retrievers love to retrieve. When you try something for the first time, and you find yourself pretty good at it, people say, "Why, he takes to that like a duck to water." What they are saying is, "He must be designed to do it; it's in his nature."

Have you ever tried something that didn't come naturally, and even after you practiced and pushed yourself, it was still difficult and felt unnatural? That tells you that it isn't in your nature, and it isn't in God's agenda for you. Drop it and move on.

Have you ever watched hunting dogs? We have a pack of noisy hunting dogs that, unfortunately, lives a block from us. You can hear them for forty miles. During the day, they usually lay around in their pens, lazy and unmotivated. But when their master backs up his truck to their cages, those dogs go berserk. Ears perk up, and they leap to attention and bark up a storm. They come alive! Their energy is unbounded. Why? Because they're going hunting. It's in their nature. God wired them for that. You know they're born to hunt when you see these ordinarily docile dogs come alive as they're released into the environment for which God designed them.

The same thing will happen to you when you find the environment and the calling God determined for you. You might have a job, an occupation, but you're not living a dream; you're living an eight-hour-a-day obligation. Do you even like your job? Or do you get up, grudgingly go to work, come home, go to sleep, and start the same thing over again the next day? It shouldn't be that way. That's not living a dream; that's living a nightmare and dying slowly.

Employees don't do their employers favors when they grudgingly take jobs, accept the money, and yet have to be coerced into false enthusiasm. If your boss is begging you, "Please be excited. Please be excellent. Please be passionate. Please love what you do," then you're not working where you're supposed to be. Your pain is transparent if you greet customers and co-workers with a frown, and recite flatly, "Nice to see you today."

> Pointless regulations and meaningless discipline lead nowhere. Discipline comes from vision. With vision and discipline, you'll discover your true, God-given *potential.*

Do you hate your job and dread going to work? Maybe you ought to reexamine your calling. When you operate out of your natural gifts and calling, work can be a joyful, rewarding experience. Remember, God will always lead you to a fulfilling destiny. Continue to be faithful and diligent; continue to ask God to open doors of opportunity that will lead you into a better understanding of His purpose for you.

## Your Passion—God's Calling

The institution of religion, not your relationship with God, might try to put you in a place that you're not designed for. If you marry a preacher, God help you! It's no easy road, believe me, because you might feel that you need to acquire a certain "preacher's wife" demeanor and manner, and shout a lot of hallelujahs. You might feel pressured to play the piano or organ, teach the ladies' Bible class, and take on responsibilities that might not be your calling.

I have good news; you won't find those rules in the Bible! Peter's wife didn't preach at all. I know he was married, because he had a mother-in-law. We have no record that any of the disciples' wives preached, sang or led Bible studies. We know that Lydia did. We know that a number of women are preachers, but why is it that a woman married to a preacher is supposed to be gifted in ministry when ministry might not be compatible with her gifts and calling?

The most phenomenal women's Bible teacher I know is Sandy Ross. She has been teaching for over 26 years. God moved her from her living room where she taught a small group of ladies to our sanctuary where she teaches hundreds of women. It's in her nature. It's easy for her. It's her God-given gift, and she loves it.

I hope my wife will acknowledge that I have never pressed her to minister beyond her gifts. Instead, I encourage her to do what comes naturally to her—what fits her comfortably and flows beautifully out of her. That way, she's happy and I'm happy. Because we all know that if mama's not happy, nobody's happy! And yet, organized religion often forces folks to comply with customs that might not necessarily fall within their gifts. Such demands cause stress, unhappiness, and even divorce. They cause people not to be at their best for God. Ultimately, many blame God, but God didn't do it. Religion did it.

Are my children supposed to become missionaries because I am a preacher? Of course not, unless they hear God's calling. I'm not a missionary. You won't find me under a mosquito net somewhere. If there's no mall and no dry cleaner, I'm not going, because it isn't in my nature. I hold missionaries in the highest regard. We support missionaries and my church sends missionaries abroad, but I'm not one who goes. God didn't make me a missionary. If He had, I would have relished a life where air conditioning, electricity and toilets are nonexistent. *Where do I go next?* I would cheerfully ask. But for that to happen, I'd have to get a new vision.

> God isn't going to make you do something you don't have a passion to do.

God isn't going to make me or you do something we hate. God isn't going to make you do something you don't have a passion to do. Some of you were never taught that and today you're in bondage. Today, you can be set free. You need to understand that the nature of a person is a powerful clue to their calling.

Marsha Sinetar wrote a book, "Do What You Love And The Money Will Follow." This is a secular book, but I want you to see a principle. The world is sometimes smarter than a believer. In Luke 16:8 says, "The children in this world are wiser in their generation than the children of light." Sinetar doesn't give God credit for her theory, but her book actually supports a Biblical principle. This book is exciting to Christians because it lends further evidence to the idea that God made you to succeed in life. Sinetar and others who have studied the business world have figured out that if you do what you love, resources will follow and you will be successful.

Many Christians believe if they do what God says, they'll be miserable. Not true. God won't take a guy who has a piano, a guitar, a powerful sound system, thousands of

CDs and a gift for composing music' and make him a postman. Some of you have an image that if you serve God, the fun is over. You think, "I will have to go to Pakistan and be an all-suffering missionary if I give my life to God." Not unless you *want* to go to Pakistan and you *want* to be a missionary!

God isn't the reason you're unhappy in your job. He isn't going to make you do things that He hasn't wired you to do. He rejoices when you make the right choice for your life.

A golfer named Dave Pelz aspired to be a PGA golf pro. When he discovered how tough the competition was, he knew he would never be another Tiger Woods or Jack Nicholas. He realized he could not make a living as a golf pro, because the odds were against him. But because golf was his life passion, he went at the game from another angle. He began following the pros on tour, studying every shot they hit—tracking their distance, accuracy and club selection. He compiled impressive data on all that it takes to be a great golfer.

After awhile, players noticed this guy always following them, and asked what he was doing. When they found out he had this arsenal of intelligence, they started seeking his counsel. Pelz showed them where they were losing ground, and why they weren't making more money on the tour. The pros took his advice, improved their games, and started paying him for his expertise. Eventually, he published, "Dave Pelz Short Game Bible," and "Dave Pelz Putting Bible." So for you golf lovers, when you're reading one of these books and your wife asks, "*What are you doing?*" you can say, "*I'm reading my Bible.*"

The point is, here's a guy who found a way to make his passion work for him.

Some of you have to recognize that the passion God put in you might not qualify you for your exact dream, but your calling might be in a related field. Like Pelz, you can stay in your passion, and be successful, prosperous and happy. God's purpose is nestled in all that comes naturally to you.

I watched an interview with Tiger Woods about three years ago. He has such electricity. He is a phenomenon. The interviewer asked him, "How do you do what you do?" Tiger got frustrated trying to explain it. He said, "I practice, and I do this and do that, but everybody practices." He finally said to the guy, "I don't know. It's just a gift."

The pros who make their jobs look easy might not know why they're successful. But I know, and God knows. It's in their nature. God wired it in. How can somebody be unprepared and still be good at what they do? It's in their nature. God made them that way.

A hostess who needs two weeks' notice to have dinner guests in her home might not have the gift of hospitality. When you have the gift and your husband brings three people home unannounced, your husband and you welcome your guests with warmth and sincerity. You cheerfully microwave a can of chili con carne, offer a dish of ice cream, and delight them with your hospitality. That's a gift . . . and it's probably also a sign of a good marriage!

### Key #5: Your purpose and calling coincide with your gifts and abilities.

Owls are nocturnal; they can see at night. Why? God designed them that way so that they can hunt in the dark. Woodpeckers can't see at night but they have strong beaks. Why? Because their gift allows them to penetrate the bark and eat insects that are burrowed in the wood. That's how they survive.

In the film, "Chariots of Fire," a Scotsman named Erik Little was a gifted runner. He's called to be a missionary, to go to China with his sister Jenny and run a mission post. He's eager to respond to God's call, but he also wants to use his gift for running and compete in the Olympics.

Eric understood that God made him for a purpose and he says that when he runs he feels God's pleasure. He tries to explain that running is a way of dedicating himself to the Lord, and says, "To win is to honor Him." This inspiring film demonstrates how a gift and a calling can coincide when in 1924, he accomplishes his Olympics goal.

"Chariots of Fire" was acclaimed as one of the best movies of the year in 1962. I highly recommend it. *"When I run, I feel God's pleasure,"* Eric said. This young man had two callings: to run to honor God, and to be a missionary to honor God. He believed that he would be holding God in contempt if he didn't use the gift of running that God gave him.

Every NBA and NFL athlete, every businessman, every housewife raising children, every minister and teacher should apply Eric Little's philosophy, "To win is to honor

Him. When I do what I have been gifted and equipped to do, I feel good about it." Think what the world could be.

Over the years, I've met many professional athletes who were fine Christian men. Uncertain about whether they're serving God by playing football or basketball, several have asked me if they should leave their sports and become preachers. I advise them that if they honestly hear God's call, they should respond, but be certain.

To stop doing what God designed you to do isn't honoring God. You could be setting yourself up for disappointment and failure, because He didn't design you to be a pastor. He wants you to be a witness through what you already do successfully. So keep running that football. Keep shooting those baskets.

> When you find the thing you're created to do, you will feel God's pleasure.

Keep being excellent at what you're designed to do; that is your platform for honoring God. You'll help young people who emulate you as a role model and who come to Christ because of you. And when you do it, when you find the thing you're created to do, you'll feel God's pleasure. It doesn't matter if you're taking care of your home and family, preaching a sermon, teaching a class, parking a car, selling insurance or writing books. When you do it because He made you to do it, you feel His pleasure.

George Foreman is a world boxing champion and a preacher in Houston. He runs an orphanage, a boys' home and a church. He appeared on the David Letterman Show, and Letterman asked, *"George, how can you be a preacher and a fighter?"* George, who has a formidable presence, assumed a mock fighting posture and said, *"Hold my Bible and I'll show you."*

George can preach and witness, and he can fight, too, because God made him that way. See the principle? When people who do what they are designed to do, it looks easy because God equips us with gifts that coincide with our purpose.

### Key #6: God provides for His purpose, not your plans.

Many people are engaged in work that God never called them to do, and they beg Him to pay the bills. But resources follow your God-given assignment, not your misguided direction. If you're not doing what He designed and assigned you to do, don't look to Him to provide for your choice.

If a preacher starts a church and ten years later the church hasn't grown and is up to its eyeballs in debt, it might be time to rethink whether or not the call to preach is your rightful calling. Honest, sincere people can make mistakes and get off track. If you're preaching, but no one is listening or following you, you probably aren't leading in the realm to which God has called you. The same thinking applies to any plan that goes awry. If you're not successful in a role you thought was supposed to be your calling, maybe you need to ask God to guide you.

Churches, unfortunately, are often a way station for Christians who don't know their callings and drift into ministry because their mothers or their denominations urged them to do so. But they ought to be elsewhere. God wants them elsewhere. If they're not happy doing ministry, they look unhappy and are ineffective. The same thinking applies to any line of work and service. If you're not called, you won't be happy and effective.

I wish people would speak honestly of this in the church. If people in business, education, military and industry can recognize clearly when they're not in the right place or can tell others they're not in the right place, why can't we be honest and recognize this in the church? Why can't we see that resources follow assignment?

Ask God to show you what He made you to do and then you will bear fruit, find pleasure and enjoy the sweet taste of success. In John 15:8, Jesus says, "My Father is glorified when you bear much fruit and become my disciples."

Heed God and resources will follow. Otherwise, you'll go nowhere in a hurry. In the church I pastor, God has been with us every step of the way, confirming our purpose as we have transitioned from renting to purchasing to constructing our own building. We are listening to Him and doing what He has called us to do.

If everything I attempted ended in failure, I would see that we were off course and I would stop. I would say, "Let's have mercy on these people and do something else! Let's shut the door and make this place a car dealership or something." But God has shown Himself to be with us, and so we remain faithful to our calling.

You don't have to hire an agent or toot your own horn to have your gifts recognized. Proverbs 18:16 reveals, "A man's gift makes room for him." When God puts His gift in you, your job is to serve and be faithful, no matter where you're planted. Do your best. You won't rely on business cards, phone calls, resumes or trumpets to announce your arrival. Serve humbly and be faithful, and your promotion will come from God. Never say, *"Hey, don't you know who I am? I'm the next Darlene Zschech! I should be singing solos!"* No, no, no—that's not how promotion comes. Be patient. Be faithful. Be a servant. Your job is to be faithful; God's job is to bring opportunity.

Serve humbly, be faithful and your promotion will come from God.

Serve as David served. He was destined to be a king, but he began by serving. He didn't act like a candidate for king. He didn't try to get an endorsement in a caucus. He didn't promote himself. He just served, and God brought him to kingship. Joseph just served—and his gift made room for him. Everywhere he was placed, people saw his gift and promoted him. Finally, when Pharaoh saw his gift, he made him ruler over Egypt.

Listen to what God says, "The gift will make room for you" Proverbs 18:16. Psalm 75:6 reveals that Promotion comes from the Lord. Let Him push you. Don't push yourself up because He might push you out of the way. Someone will notice your talent and willingness, and news will soon reach the top. Proverbs 22:29 promises, "See a man diligent in his business, he shall stand before kings. He won't stand before obscurity."

Most people get it wrong. They think, "I want to meet important people." But God is saying to you, "Be diligent where you're planted in business." God will see to it that you stand before important people.

Glen Campbell started as a studio musician and master guitarist. Occasionally, he was asked to sing backup with recording stars. He also wrote songs that became other people's hits. Ultimately, his gift made room for him, and he became a standout artist who performs his own music. Use what God has put in you, and eventually, inevitably God's promotion will find you.

### Key #7: Learn to soar with your strengths and manage your weaknesses.

Men, if you can't handle money well, but your wife has a gift for administration or she is a trained accountant, let her manage your money. You make it. Let her manage it. Just because you can make it doesn't mean you can manage it. You might protest, "But I am head of my home." Yes, but you're not an accountant. Your family will go bankrupt if you can't handle the money. A professional athlete might make big money on the basketball court, but spend it all before he gets home. If his wife is a good steward, he should let her manage his weakness. Then he is freed up to soar with his strengths. He makes it; she manages it. They are both blessed and their home is blessed.

We should direct everyone, especially children, to pursue their strengths, not their weaknesses. A friend tells me, "My son Billy can't pass a math test. It's hard and he hates it. He cries about it and can't make good grades in math . . . but he makes As and Bs in literature and art." So what do the average parents do? They give him more math! They give their children more of what they're not designed to do. They think that by doing this, their children will improve.

Obviously, we have to help our children get through required courses and do the best they can do. But if we're going to push them, then push them toward their strengths, toward those classes where good grades come easily. Keep pushing them down that road because that's a clue to their identity and a clue to God's purpose in them.

You're thinking, "But I want my kid to go to college." I understand; I treasure my college education, and encourage every young person to value education. But realistically, college isn't for everyone. Some young people are better served when they can pursue a specialty education in an area of their strength.

Let your child follow his path and he might be paying *your* bills in ten years. Encourage him to discover God's purpose for him, and he will rise to a level that surpasses your expectations. Graduating from college doesn't guarantee success. There are college graduates who are starving to death. We should focus on educating our children in the areas of their passions and excellence, in the areas that come naturally to them; and they will succeed.

Romans 12:6 tells us to find what we do well, and do more of it, and learn to manage our weakness. I am a leader. I love to cast visions. I love to exhort people to achieve their dreams, to get out of their comfort zones and go for it. I know that is in me and I am happiest when I'm living out my passion.

On the other hand, I dislike meetings, financial statements, interviews and counseling. I'm not a counselor. It makes me miserable; the very idea makes me want to run and hide. So I tell my church staff, "Let's work as a family and as a team. Let me cast a vision and then let somebody else do the administration." And if that isn't a job to them, but a gift, they'll perform with passion. They'll get a warm fuzzy feeling doing that which I dislike doing. The church will be stronger because of it and I'll be freed up to do what I'm called and equipped to do. The whole church family will find excellence, passion and productivity.

No pastor can do it all. One of our staff pastors does an excellent job working with the new members' class in our church. If we took him away, it would be a disaster. The reason he excels at that job is because of his gifting. Personally, I don't want to do it. If my wife said, "*Today we are going to be teaching the new members' class for four hours,*" I would rather get a root canal instead!

Churches, schools, families and societies have been operating illogically for generations putting people in the wrong places, assigning tasks to those who are not gifted to do them, and wondering why things aren't working! When you realize that God has surrounded you with people who are gifted to do things that you're not, you learn to delegate your weaknesses. You soar with your strengths. It's a concept that works in business, marriage, families and churches. It works in life. So let's do it!

Romans 12:6 says, "*God has given each of us the ability to do certain things.*" Note the phrase *certain things*, not *everything*. If God has given you the ability to prophesy, don't join the choir. Instead, speak out with your faith and know that God is speaking through you. If your gift is that of serving others, serve them well. If you're a teacher, teach with excellence. If your gift is to encourage others, cheer them on. If you have money, share it generously.

God expects me to continue to learn as a preacher and strive always to do a better job, and He also expects you to learn and strive in your area of giftedness.

Find your gift and use it eagerly, passionately, capably.

If God gave you the gift to make money, make lots of it! Benefit yourself, but use the excess for the kingdom. That's your spiritual job, just as preaching is mine. If God has given you leadership ability, take the responsibility seriously. If you have a gift for showing kindness to others, do it gladly. Find your gift and use it eagerly, passionately, and capably.

Mark Twain wrote a story about a man who spent his entire life searching for the world's greatest general. He never found him. Finally the man died and went to heaven. St. Peter greeted him. (This is obviously not good theology, but it's a powerful story.) The man said to St. Peter, "I am looking for the world's greatest general."

Peter said, "Come with me."

In a few minutes, St. Peter pointed out a man and said, "There's the world's greatest general."

The man said to Peter, "You must be mistaken. That man was a blacksmith in my hometown."

Peter said, "That is true, but if he had been a general, he would have been the world's greatest general."

When I read Mark Twain's story, something snapped in me. *"I wonder what could have been?"* will be written on some of our tombstones because we were afraid; we were comfortable and unmotivated. We missed out on our destinies because we didn't follow our passions, the nature of our gifting, the purposes for which God designed us. I wonder who could have built the greatest church, who could have established the most successful business, who could have reared children who would have changed the world? I wonder who could have cured cancer, ended human conflict, and discovered the key to world peace?

Don't live a life; live a dream. Live a passion. Live a destiny. Don't let your dream die in you. Life is too short. The kingdom is too precious, and the need too great. Find the thing God made you to do—the thing that makes you joyful when you do it. Give yourself to it with all your heart. Glorify God with it and when you do, you will feel blessed and your soul will soar.

## Amazing Keys to Your Potential

- God's purpose for you preceded His creation of you.

- Your purpose determines your design.

- Your purpose predicts your potential.

- God's purpose is nestled neatly in your nature.

- Your purpose and calling coincide with your gifts and abilities.

- God provides for His purpose, not your plans.

- Manage your weaknesses, and learn to soar with your strengths.

# —5—

# Overcoming Your Negative Past

Whatever is happening in your life right now and wherever you are, you have gifts and abilities that can make you fruitful and productive. When God sees that you're using His gifts wisely, graciously and generously, He will anoint you and make you forget the pain that haunts you from your past. But first, before God can deliver you from the land of your affliction, you must be productive and excellent. I am here to walk with you as you begin your journey.

A friend of mine, a young man in his mid-20s, recently received two lungs from a donor. He was born with an incurable lung disease. Without the transplant, he was going to die. In his land of affliction, he could have just rolled over and died. He had never been able to take a full breath of air. He always had an oxygen tank at his side; he had been frequently hospitalized; he was susceptible to any germ or respiratory infection. He never enjoyed the peace of good health.

Yet, in spite of his affliction, he didn't get a handicap permit for his car. He came to church; he was active; he served; he gave; and he worked. He engaged life in his affliction and was fruitful. He was productive. He didn't sit around and wait; he kept living, working and serving year after year. And God favored him with this gift of new lungs. He didn't say, "When I get some lungs, I'll come to church. When I get my lungs and get my life right, I'll honor the Lord and get involved."

Instead, he got involved in the midst of being afflicted. He got involved near death, not knowing if he would live one more year. What must it be like to awaken from this miraculous surgery and do what I take for granted every day—take a full breath of air.

Instead of waiting for God to change his circumstance, my friend became fruitful and productive in the midst of great affliction. He sowed himself, becoming fruitful and productive. Then, his circumstance changed. He received newly transplanted lungs, and with God's grace, he will have a better quality of life and live a long time.

Through my friend's story, seen in the light of two biblical characters—Joseph and David, we will discover

God's remarkable principles for overcoming our negative pasts.

## Be Fruitful Then Forget the Pain

In the story of Joseph and the naming of his sons—Ephraim and Manasseh—we discover an important message for our own lives. Through the metaphor of Ephraim and Manasseh, we see how God blessed Israel, and how God will bless us. Israel experienced Ephraim first, before Manasseh came. God said something like, "I am going to bless you. First, I will first make you productive; I will make you fruitful. Then, I will anoint you. You will forget the pain of your father's house."

Genesis 41 narrates the story of Joseph—a man of God's infinite blessing, a man who overcame his negative past. Like Joseph, many of us are born with some deficit, affliction or disability. We inherit certain things we don't choose. Think of your own life. You didn't choose your parents, your siblings, or your race. You didn't choose the social conditions into which you were born. All of these were bequeathed to you. If you had chosen, would you have chosen differently?

If your life has been burdened with damaging baggage from your past, do you have to carry that baggage forever? God says, "No." What a grave mistake to resign yourself to the past. Turn to God and He will give you the power to overcome your past by transforming your life and your future into an incredible blessing.

Joseph's background was a series of unjust and brutal events that began with the savage conduct of his own brothers. First, he was kidnapped, sold into slavery in

Egypt, falsely accused of a crime and thrown into jail. But Joseph's life demonstrates the power of persistence, courage, productivity, dreams and forgiveness. His story is all the more inspiring because he developed his amazing character despite the pain, trouble and jealousy wrought by his family.

> ——— • ◆ • ———
>
> It's possible to overcome and change your negative past— God has the power to trans- form your life into an incredible blessing.
>
> ——— • ◆ • ———

As one of twelve brothers, Joseph's life was marked with conflict and rivalry. Joseph exhibited signs of superiority that fueled his brothers' jealousy. In a family of underachievers, he was a boy with dreams. He wasn't content to settle for the limitations of his birth family. He had a vision of great- ness for his life, and because of it, he was destined for trouble.

No one will give you trouble if you live complacently and without dreams. But if you dare to dream beyond your present reality, you're a threat to those who have no dreams. You might think present reality is the way it always will be, but you're wrong. If you think that way, woe to the person who dares to dream in your pres- ence because like Joseph's brothers, you become a dream- killer when you fail to believe in the power of dreams.

Joseph was a dreamer who suffered his brothers' wrath even though he didn't really do anything wrong. His biggest mistake was shooting off his mouth to those envious brothers. He paid a big price for his youthful boasting.

## Don't Reverse God's Process for Overcoming Your Negative Past

"During this time, before the arrival of the first of the famine years, two sons were born to Joseph and his wife. Joseph named his older son Manasseh, for he said, God has made me forget all my troubles and the household of my father. Joseph named his second son Ephraim, for he said, God has made me fruitful in the land of my affliction" (Genesis 41:50-51).

Two sons were born to Joseph at a good time in his life. He had been released from slavery and imprisonment. He came a long way from the days of having a dream and then being persecuted and rejected by his brothers, sold into slavery, and ultimately thrown into jail. In this passage, we find him as the ruler of Egypt. His dream had come true and he had two sons, Manasseh and Ephraim.

But Joseph had things backwards when he named his sons. He had it all wrong. He didn't understand the order and process in the way God works. I'll tell you where Joseph erred.

He named his firstborn *Manasseh*, a word that means, "to cause to forget." It means, "to be delivered and released from the painful memory of a negative past." When Joseph named *Manasseh*, he had already been released from the consequences of his past. His brothers had sold him into slavery, but God had turned life to his advantage. Joseph called it "the state of forgetting."

Forgetting doesn't mean you have no recollection. It means that the events of the past no longer influence you, even though you might remember them. There is no more pain. You don't forget, but when you remember, it's a distant memory that doesn't trouble you. So Joseph said, "*God has caused me to forget my past.*" God delivered Joseph from his father's house and all the pain, rejection, envy, jealousy and strife he endured there.

> ———— •◆• ————
>
> God will make you prosperous, productive and fruitful in the land of your affliction.
>
> ———— •◆• ————

The second son is named Ephraim. Ephraim means *"fruitful, productive, prosperous."* Joseph gave him this name because "God has made me prosperous, productive and fruitful in the land of my affliction." Not delivered from affliction, but right in the middle what was negative, wrong, and had caused the most pain, God made Joseph fruitful. God will make you prosperous, productive and fruitful in the land of your affliction.

We expect just the opposite. We pray, "God get me out of my affliction, and then I will be fruitful." We think that we must be completely healed, restored and set free before anything productive can happen in our lives. The truth is, we can begin to prosper in the midst of pain. We can move forward, no matter what obstacles might lie in our path.

Joseph's story illustrates that our locations or situations in life do not limit us, because God's will changes everything. He can move you from your father's house to unfamiliar territory, and then bless you in the new land of uncertainty. It isn't likely that Joseph would have gone to Egypt by his own choice, but God used his brothers' evil, malicious kidnapping to achieve the transformation.

If Joseph had not gone to this foreign land, he would have remained a nomad, keeping sheep. Not much of a future out there in the fields! We would never have read about him in the Bible.

When you leave the safety and familiarity of your past to enter the uncertainty of your future, you're driven to do far more than when you were comfortable in your father's house. Throughout history, folks who migrated from one land to another generally came out ahead. America was settled primarily by immigrants who were looking for a better life. In large measure, they got it.

> Joseph's story illustrates that we are not limited by our location or situation in life, because God will change everything.

Joseph mistakenly thought that the sequence of his life and the deliverance from his negative past happened this way: First, Manasseh—*God delivered me from my past.* Second, Ephraim—*God will make me productive and now fruitful.* That's how Joseph saw it. But Joseph was wrong. Let me prove it to you.

## Prosperity (Ephraim) Comes First!

Joseph put Manasseh first. He misunderstood how God had really worked in his life. He saw forgetfulness coming before prosperity—Ephraim. He mistakenly thought as many of us do. We imagine that God will completely deliver us from pain, and miraculously help us forget our pasts, and then, we'll become productive and prosperity. But God's way is just the opposite of what we think!

Joseph's father, Jacob, understood the ways of God. We read in Genesis 48 that the day came when Jacob was old and about to die. So Joseph took his sons, Manasseh and Ephraim, to his father for a blessing. When Joseph brought his sons to Jacob, here is the essence of what Jacob said, "Joseph, God Almighty appeared to me at Luz in the land of Canaan and blessed me. He said to me—I will make you a multitude of nations and I will give this land of Canaan to you and your descendants as an everlasting possession. Now I am adopting as my own sons these two boys of yours, Ephraim and Manasseh, who were born here in the land of Egypt before I arrived. They will inherit from me just as Ruben and Simeon will."

Remember, Joseph saw the process of his life as Manasseh coming first, then Ephraim: God will deliver me from my past; then He will make me productive and fruitful. But look at what Jacob did! He reversed Joseph's order for his sons. When Jacob, his father, recounted the story, he changed the sequence. Instead of saying Manasseh and Ephraim, he says Ephraim and Manasseh. Why did Jacob change the order?

Let's look more closely at this story in Genesis 48:8-9, 13-14: "Then Jacob looked over at the two boys. 'Are these your sons,' he asked. 'Yes,' Joseph told him. 'Yes, these are the sons God has given me here in Egypt.' Jacob said, 'Bring them over to me and I will bless them . . . .' Then, Joseph positioned the boys so that Ephraim was at Jacob's left hand and Manasseh was at his right hand. But Jacob crossed his arms as he reached out to lay his hands on the boys' heads So that his right hand was on the head of Ephraim, the younger boy, and his left hand was on the head of Manasseh, the older boy" (NLT).

In ancient Israel, the right hand was the symbol of favor, power, blessing and double portion. It was a greater blessing than the left hand. So when Joseph took the two boys in front of their grandfather Jacob, he lined them up in their birth order—Manasseh in front of Jacob's right hand and Ephraim in front of the left hand.

Jacob changed the order! He crossed his two hands, and put his right hand on the younger boy and his left hand on the older son. Scripture says he did it knowingly.

Remember, Joseph assumed that one must experience Manasseh—deliverance first, before you experience Ephraim—productivity, fruitfulness and prosperity.

So when Jacob reversed the order, what did Joseph do? Genesis 48:17-20 NLT reads,

> But Joseph was upset when he saw that his father had laid his right hand on Ephraim's head. So he lifted it to place it on Manasseh's head instead. "No, Father," he said, "this one over here is older. Put your right hand on his head."
> But his father refused. "I know what I'm doing, my son," he said. "Manasseh, too, will become a great people, but his younger brother will become even greater. His descendants will become a multitude of nations!" So Jacob blessed the boys that day with this blessing: "The people of Israel will use your names to bless each other. They will say, 'Might God make you as prosperous as Ephraim and Manasseh.' "In this way, Jacob put Ephraim ahead of Manasseh.

God is giving us insight into overcoming and conquering our negative pasts. Jacob said that this was how Israel would be blessed. They would experience Ephraim first, before Manasseh came. God said, "If I am going to bless you, I will first make you productive. I will make you fruitful. And when I make you fruitful and productive, then you will forget the pain of your father's house." Joseph was thinking that God would deliver him first, and then make him productive and fruitful.

You know how it is. We think, "As soon as I get a better job and make more money, I will sharpen up, put on some makeup, drop a few pounds, work harder, and be excellent. But right now, I'm in a minimum wage job, and I'm not putting out too much. I am waiting on my deliverance." But Manasseh will never come unless you're fruitful and productive right where you are.

If you don't lose the weight now, sharpen up now, wash that hair more than once a week, put on a little makeup and live your life in excellence, you'll never see deliverance because that promotion will never come.

This is contrary to the way most people think. Today, most people think, "God will cause me to forget my past, my pain, my toil, my rejection, my hurt, and my poverty, and will deliver me from the affliction of my father's house. Then, He will make me fruitful." But these people are mistakenly looking for deliverance before productivity.

So, they sit down and wait for God to deliver them. But God's way isn't to deliver you first from your negative past. First, He makes you productive and fruitful. When you become fruitful and productive, that fruitfulness will encourage promotion, and cause you to forget the pain of your past. So God's plan is Ephraim first, then Manasseh.

God is saying to you right now, "I will bless you with fruitfulness and productivity; then you will begin to forget the pain of your past."

Remember, we all inherit some problems, challenges, and deficits in life—conditions over which we have no control. There are people waiting, expecting their problems to be solved before they get on with their lives. They want to experience Manasseh, deliverance, before Ephraim, becoming productive and fruitful.

> If you don't lose the weight now, sharpen up now, wash that hair more than once a week, put on a little makeup and live your life in excellence, you will never see deliverance because that promotion will never come.

Yet, God is saying, "If you expect Manasseh before Ephraim, you won't be productive and fruitful in life." In the midst of your affliction, God says, "I will make you fruitful first and when I bless you, your past will no longer influence you." If you don't experience productivity and fruitfulness, your past will haunt you the rest of your life.

## Start Now and Be Productive

Let's discover how this worked in the life of another well-known biblical character, David the shepherd boy. 1 Samuel 17 tells the story of David and Goliath. 1 Samuel 17:23-26 reads,

*And as he was talking to them, he saw Goliath, the champion from Gath, come out from the Philistine ranks, shouting his challenge to the army of Israel. As soon as the Israelite army saw him, they began to run away in fright. Have you seen the giant? the men were asking. He comes out each day to challenge Israel.* [Then David's ears perked up.] *And have you heard about the huge reward the king is offering to anybody who kills him? The king will give him one of his daughters for a wife and his whole family will be exempted from paying taxes.* [Who could resist that? Tax-free living!] *David talked to others standing there to verify the report. Is that true? What will a man get for killing this Philistine giant and putting an end to his abuse of Israel, he asked. Who is this pagan Philistine anyway that he is allowed to defy the armies of the living God?*

———— • ◆ • ————

Risky, hard work doesn't set well with complaining, whining people, like religious church folks today, who want deliverance first.

———— • ◆ • ————

Notice the three things that would happen to the man who killed Goliath. First, he would become rich. Second, he would marry the king's daughter. Third, his family would enjoy a tax-free exemption. Here was David. For a poor boy to become rich; for a nobody shepherd to marry the daughter of a king—a princess; for a man with debt to become tax-free, the condition was: *kill a giant.* Risky, hard work doesn't set well with complaining, whining people, like religious church folks today, who want deliverance first. They want to win the Lotto. They want all their problems to vanish. They think, "I'm a Christian. I shouldn't be having problems." The truth is, everyone will face a giant at one time or another.

Nobody wants to kill a giant. Until you're able to kill a giant as David did, you can't experience deliverance from your poverty and the ordinariness of your past. If you don't take your giant down, you're going back to the desert, to your minimum wage job and your stinking sheep. We will never know your name. You must put Ephraim before Manasseh.

So how was David going to kill Goliath? How was he going to be productive? How was he going to be fruitful? One thing I know is, he was limited to the tools he had: a slingshot and a stone. That's all he was issued on the backside of a desert. Goliath was a trained military combat soldier. He had a shield, a spear and full body armor. David had only a slingshot, but he had been throwing stones for years at lions, bears and other wild animals that preyed on his dad's sheep.

Often when we face our Goliaths, our giants, our negative pasts, we are so overwhelmed by the size of the problems that we soon forget what we have. I could write a book on what I don't have, but I forget what I do have. God gives everybody something. We all have something.

> I could write a book on what I don't have, but I forget what I do have. God gives everybody something.

Nothing happened in the battle until David came onto the scene—a young man who had confidence in his weapon. He could throw stones. He developed his skill, so he was confident, not cocky. He was confident he could take this giant down.

How did David develop his skill? Why had he been working with it for years, doing mundane things in obscurity and rejection?

Nobody believed in him; nobody saw potential in him. His father rejected him; his brothers rejected him. He wasn't born with a silver spoon in his mouth. Even the prophet who came to pick a new king for Israel didn't see his potential. This boy didn't have a chance—no references or referrals. But he could do one thing. He probably thought, "My life is going nowhere. All I can do out here is hit that coyote."

That is what Daddy told him to do, and he did it. No paycheck—just a little bowl of soup at the end of the day and a flock of sheep for company. He didn't get to sit down with an instructor and take a few music lessons, write some songs and enjoy his youth. The boy had a hard life. No future. No princess. No wealth. He didn't see a throne, and nobody saw him. But what he did, he did with confidence, expertise, and proficiency. He threw stones. Had been doing that for years. It was a boring job, but he had done it with excellence.

The Bible says the tribe of Benjamin had several hundred men who were such good shots with a sling that they could hit a reed at 100 meters. With a rock—now that's accuracy! That's like a sniper with a scope. That was the potential in this army of Israel, but they forgot what they had when faced with the enormity of the giant. On the other hand, David decided something like this, "That skill I have been developing in obscurity is going to pay me rich dividends." God didn't hurl the stone David picked up. The Holy Spirit did not direct the stone at the giant and fell the mighty brute. It didn't happen that way.

David knew he could hit Goliath because he had been developing his skill. When they offered him other weapons, he said in summary, "I haven't been trained with those and don't know how to use them. Just give me my slingshot and my stone. I am confident." Goliath, who was a skilled warrior, had only one unprotected spot. In his full body armor, only his forehead was vulnerable. So this couldn't be a lucky shot. It had to be skilled and sure.

When God raises someone from nothingness to greatness, people might stand in awe and say, "Oh, look what the Lord hath done. He picked up a lazy, do-nothing, be nothing person and made him a star." It doesn't happen this way, and it didn't happen that way with Joseph. He was a man of excellent administration, faithfulness and moral conduct and that's why God elevated him. In spite of the afflictions in his path, Joseph became excellent, faithful and moral. With David, God didn't say, "I just need somebody to throw a rock. Anyone will do." He needed a skilled marksman who could hit that giant directly on the forehead. David had skill, courage and confidence, so God used him.

God can't use somebody who can't do anything. David was the only candidate on the spot who knew what to do and how to do it. David must have thought something like this, "*I can do this, I can do this, I CAN do this! I have been doing this for years—for minimum wage at a fast food burger joint. I can do this! Hold the mayo, no onions. I can do this. I can do this.*" David seized the day. With his hand-fashioned slingshot, he slung that rock smack into the enemy's forehead, and knocked him unconscious. David severed the giant's head with his own sword.

1 Samuel 17:50 reads, "*David prevailed over the Philistine Giant with a stone and sling.*" It doesn't say the Holy Spirit lit up his hairdo and a host of angels flew around him and the Lord. It says David prevailed because he knew how to use his skill and this was the pay-off: he was fruitful against the giant. He learned to be fruitful and productive on the battlefield, in the land of affliction against Goliath. Then, he reaped the rewards—a wife, riches and tax-free living.

## God's Process for Change: Ephraim First, Then Manasseh

Do you get the moral of Joseph's and David's stories? If you want to forget your negative past and conquer it, you begin by being productive and using your skills and abilities to achieve victory right where you are. When you achieve victory, the reward of your victory helps you leave your bad memories in the dust.

> God says to you and me, "Do great things, and I will deliver you."

God says to you, "*I am going to give you Ephraim first, and after you experience Ephraim, you will get Manasseh. After you're fruitful and productive, you will forget your negative past.*" Do you see that? That is God's process for changing your life.

Lord, if you will anoint me, I will do great things for you.

God says, *Get off your lazy behind and do great things for me first, now—and then I will anoint. Sow and you will reap. Do great things, I will deliver you.*"

Even Joseph didn't correctly perceive how he was able to overcome his negative past. First, he was fruitful, despite his enslavement. He served; he organized; he practiced excellence wherever he found himself—first in Potiphar's house and then in jail. He didn't say, *"Boy oh boy, if I ever get out of jail, I will dress up and be a good leader and get rid of my negative attitude."* Instead, he showed up on time, and did everything he was told . . . and then some. He took the initiative. He identified and solved problems without being asked.

Finally, the leaders said, "Put that guy in charge. We don't need to be here anymore. He can run everything." His fruitfulness and productivity, born in affliction, got him rewarded and promoted. When he finally used his dream-interpreting skill on Pharaoh, his freedom and future were cinched. In essence, Pharaoh said, "This guy is too good to stay in prison. Get him a new Armani suit. Get him a fine car and a watch. I want him next to me. He is smarter than all the people on my staff. He doesn't belong in jail. I need him."

What came first? Productivity and fruitfulness. That's what got him promoted and rewarded. And soon he was no longer affected by his past. He was able to transcend the oppression, slavery, and rejection.

If you don't have a good attitude flipping hamburgers in a fast food franchise, you won't have a better attitude as

> ————— • ◆ • —————
>
> If you can't have a
> good attitude flip-
> ping hamburgers
> in a fast food
> franchise, you
> won't have a
> better attitude as
> CEO of the
> company.
>
> ————— • ◆ • —————

CEO of the company. It isn't going to happen. Do the best you can with what you have, or you'll continue on your negative path, even if God was to promote you. But He won't.

I challenge you with this fact: God says first Ephraim, then Manasseh. Joseph, in affliction, was fruitful and productive in using the gifts God gave him. His positive spirit and resourcefulness made a way for him and brought him before Pharaoh, who made him ruler of Egypt. He was first fruitful, Ephraim; then he was delivered, Manasseh. When Joseph's brothers came to see him years later, fearing he would retaliate against them, Joseph had been so blessed and rewarded and promoted, he held no vengeance in his heart. He didn't have any pain from his negative past. It was gone.

## The Lord Wants to Transform You Right Where You Are!

That is how God is going to do it for you. If you wait for your deliverance to come first, you might wait a long time. Deliverance might never come. If you're in a bad marriage and waiting for something to happen to make it better or end it entirely, consider this: the Lord might want to change *you*. He might want to make your marriage so good, you'll be amazed and wonder how it happened.

To start, you have to be fruitful and productive. You have to discard your anger and bitterness over disappointments and unfulfilled expectations. You don't want to work through your problems . . . it's too hard, too painful, too pointless. But guess what? While you're waiting on deliverance, you'll be sitting with your wife a long time, in misery. She could bury you, collect your insurance and marry somebody else. You would deserve it.

Why don't *you* just change? Why don't you become fruitful and productive right there in that bad marriage? If there's any hope at all for promotion, then that's how it comes. Ephraim first, then Manasseh—or you'll be bitter and unhappy all your life.

You have financial problems, and you're thinking, "Boy, if I can just get some money, I am going to pay off these bills, buy a big car, yeah, yeah, yeah." Your wife will be living with somebody else and spending your life insurance money before the fortune you're awaiting rolls in. You'll be long gone. If you want to overcome your problems, you have to be fruitful right where you are. Do you have only a little and make only a little? Then learn to be a good steward of your little.

My church knows that story. We came out of nothing. Slowly, not instantly, but slowly, God promoted us until now I have to be reminded of those days when we rented a sorry old building. I forget that we came out of a wretched chapter in our history when the future seemed hopeless and we had nothing to keep us going but pure faith. It isn't a painful memory, because it seems

> Do not cry. "Lord, anoint me and I will do great things for you." God says," Do great things for me and then I will anoint you."

so far removed from today. That's because we remained fruitful in spite of a negative situation, and the Lord anointed us. Do not cry, "Lord, anoint me and I will do great things for you." God says, "Do great things for me and then I will anoint you."

## Use What God Has Given You *NOW*

Don't wait. God isn't going to solve your problem. You must begin using what He has given you. God doesn't respond to self-pity. He responds to obedience. You won't attract His attention until you comply with the eternal, immutable principles He has ordained.

Here's an example. You've got a grain of corn and you're hungry. No matter how you pray over that grain, no matter whether you spit on it or lay hands on it—that grain of corn isn't going to grow. Anointed with oil or blessed, it remains a dead piece of corn. You must be in line with God's principles. You can cry, complain and blame it on the atmosphere, the ozone layer, global warming. Believe that's why it isn't growing. But that's not it.

**What is God's principle? If you want it to grow, don't pray. Plant it!** That is the principle. Plant it, and it will grow. Sow it, and you can reap. Don't expect to receive a healing ministry before you pray for another who's sick. Learn to be a good steward and honor the Lord with your tithe and your resources. Then you'll find prosperity.

God says, *"I will give you Ephraim before you get Manasseh."* You have to become fruitful in your land of affliction before God delivers you from the effects of your past. If you want your situation to change, America to change, your marriage to change, your financial situation to change, or your health to change—you can cry and pray and cry and pray. Things might change—but only because somebody did something proactive, fruitful, and productive. Never beg or bargain, *God, if you will give me, I will . . .* No—*do something* and God will give you. Do what you can.

The difficulty lies in the land of your affliction. When afflicted, what do people most often want to do? Nothing. Nothing but complain, murmur and blame somebody else saying something like, "It's my mother's fault; it's my daddy's fault; it's the Democrats' fault; it's the Republicans' fault; it's President Bush's fault; it's my teacher's fault; it's the policeman's fault."

Consider this: *the answer might lie in the very affliction that's got you down.*

The one who's most effective in counseling battered women was likely a battered woman herself. Instead of waiting for deliverance, she became fruitful first. As she helped others, God began to deliver her from the pain of her past. If she had ceased living and giving, and had said, *"God, deliver me before I minister to others,"* she might never have been freed from her past. You can never get free from your past until you start using what God has given you in the land of your affliction.

> You can never get free from your past until you start using what God has given you in the land of your affliction.

Many new ideas and new businesses are born because frustrated employees get fed up with poor management, and say, *"Why don't I just do it myself?"* As they become productive in their affliction, they experience Manasseh. God took man out of the earth, then gave him dominion over it. God took Joseph out of his affliction of the land of Egypt, then made him ruler over it. Your struggle is your ministry. God might have taken you out of poverty because you practiced good stewardship and productivity despite your limited assets.

My first tithe check was $2.50. I can remember how small and pitiful it was against the new building we were trying to finance. I was twenty-seven years old and just beginning my march with Jesus—just beginning to learn to obey some principles in my land of affliction. I had one suit that felt like cardboard, one shirt and one tie. I had no stress in dressing at all. There was one choice. Every Sunday I wore the same suit, shirt and tie. I drove a yellow VW Super Beetle with 230,000 miles on it and no air-conditioning. I lived by myself in a 50-foot long, 10-foot wide mobile home with roaches as big as skateboards. Yes, sir. I really had a silver spoon in my mouth. But I remember saying, *"I am not going to live like this forever,"* and I started sowing with my $2.50 tithe. I showed up on time and did as good a job with what I had as could be done. I was fruitful in that miserable condition. I was productive; and that productivity ultimately brought reward.

God isn't going to put money in the bank to make you rich. You might never be able to say, "Look, honey, somebody put a million dollars in our bank account. Wow!" Sorry, but you're responsible for putting money in the bank.

Use what you have. Solve a problem. Kill a Goliath. Marry the king's daughter. Escape your negative past. Thank God for a Goliath or we would never know a David. Thank God for Egypt, racist, discriminatory, abusive, terrible Egypt, because without that experience, Joseph would have remained a broke, nomadic sheepherder, living with his parents, instead of serving as prime minister to a king, ruler of a nation. Your giant, your obstacle, your problem is a gateway to significance and promotion. God wants you to learn to be fruitful right there in your pain—right there—because it makes you a great testimony to the power and grace of God to other people.

My challenge to you is this: don't sit around anymore. Don't say, "Well, when I get my life together, I am going to become a Christian." Don't be a moron. You'll never get it together or you would have already gotten it together. You're going to have to give your life to Christ and let

> Your giant, your obstacle, your problem is a gateway to significance and promotion.

Him help you get it together or it won't happen at all. You say, "Well, when I can give $100,000, then I will step in big time."

Leave your ego at the door. Let me tell you, God would rather have your $5 now to do His work in this world than to wait for you to hit the $100,000 jackpot. Because if your heart is right, if you get $100,000, it'll be because you were generous with the $5 or the $100 or $5,000 or $50,000 you had. Use your gifts.

## Decide to Be Fruitful and Productive Right Where You Are!

If you're in a bad place, I'm trying to help you today. Remember that it's "Ephraim first, then Manasseh." Don't wait to get your life together to give it to Christ. Be productive. Make a wise choice. Today is the day of salvation. Accept Jesus and cast all your cares on Him. He will give you the power to change. Maybe you need to rededicate your life because you have lost focus, and your enemies have confused you. It's okay—be fruitful.

**Today, decide to be fruitful and productive.** Give your life, your resources to God Almighty. Put your life in His hands and watch as He makes you fruitful. Watch Him bring deliverance from your negative past. Perhaps you've been waiting for God to intervene . . . and God has been waiting for you to use what you have.

Don't wait until you're well to help another. If you're sick, pray for somebody else who's sick. If you have financial needs, do something out of your poverty to help alleviate someone else's problem. Your contribution might be small, but you can perform an act of kindness to help somebody else.

Maybe you have been addicted to drugs, and you can help an inner city ministry because you've been there and you know too well the devil's power over addiction. You're not free yet, not completely. But you can be as fruitful as Ephraim, and guarantee your deliverance.

Perhaps you came from a bad marriage or an abusive background and you want to wait until you're over all your trials before you can help somebody. Well, you'll never get over all your trials. So, start helping somebody now, in the land of your affliction.

Right now, move Manasseh aside and hug Ephraim. It's time to get up and get going. Refuse to sit around waiting for your past to be healed before you step into your potential and your future. Drop your excuses.

God is empowering you right now to overcome your negative past!

## Amazing Keys to Your Potential

1. God will make you prosperous, productive and fruitful in the land of your affliction.

2. Don't just sit and complain when you're wounded; start being productive.

3. If you want to grow, don't pray . . . sow!

4. Your obstacle or problem is your gateway to significance and promotion.

# 6

# The Kingdom of the Eighth Child

Scattered throughout the Bible, we find examples of God choosing ordinary men and women to do His work in the world. If you feel unfulfilled and unnoticed, open your heart to God, and no matter where you are, He will find you. You're God's chosen— your life is about to unfold because you're a candidate for the Kingdom of the Eighth Child.

Allow me introduce you to the Kingdom of the Eighth Child. In the Bible, the number eight is symbolic of God's new beginnings. The Kingdom of the Eighth Child and the story of David can be used as a metaphor that applies to each of us. This story symbolizes the people that others consider to be losers, but are chosen by God. These chosen comprise the "Kingdom of the Eighth Child."

In 1 Samuel 16, we read the story of the prophet Samuel visiting the house of Jesse. He came to anoint a new king for Israel. When seven of Jesse's eight sons came for Samuel's scrutiny, they looked good—handsome and stylish, and both Samuel and Jesse thought surely one of them would qualify to be king.

But as the seven sons passed in front of Jesse, God rejected them even though they all looked good to Samuel. God reminded Samuel in 1 Samuel 16:7, "Don't judge by his appearance or height, for I have rejected him. The LORD doesn't make decisions the way you do! People judge by outward appearance, but the LORD looks at a person's thoughts and intentions" (NLT).

So, God's reminder to the prophet was something like this, "Listen, Samuel, I have whispered a name in your ear, and until the son who bears that name comes, I don't care how the rest of them look outwardly. I will choose my leader by his heart and inner qualities." The eighth child, David, was in the field watching the sheep. His father, Jesse, had to send for him. He was the one that Samuel was to anoint as the next king of Israel.

## God Chooses From the Last in Line

Jesse's seven sons looked good, but God rejected them. God's quest has always been for the right man or the right woman. Most of the time, it's an inconspicuous person who has gone unnoticed by everyone else. So here's the good news—if you feel that way, inconspicuous and unnoticed, know that God chooses from the rear of the line, not the front.

David was in the back of the pack, not in front, and God sought him out and chose him. Man chooses more superficially—by appearance, talent, ability. God isn't looking for Johnny Handsome and Charlie Charismatic. God is committed to character.

> If you feel that way, inconspicuous and unnoticed, know that God chooses from the rear of the line, not the front.

Talent is given as a gift from God to you. Talent is something that flows out of you naturally; you can't conjure it up. You can enhance it, improve it, and even master it. If you can throw a football 100 yards or knock a baseball out of the field, you did nothing to merit that gift. You have an innate ability given to you at birth by the grace of God.

**Character**, on the other hand, isn't given. You have to work for it, discipline yourself, and make wise choices. Yet our culture celebrates and throws money at talent, but paying little attention to character. Parents do it. Sports are infamous for doing it. The media is the champion at celebrating talent. Our society is abundant with celebrities, with wealthy and successful people who are overpaid, with lots of talent and very little character. Our culture, even in the church, has been too quick to anoint pride, arrogance, talent and hardiness.

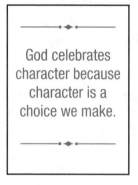

God celebrates character because character is a choice we make.

We need to encourage character in our children. We ought to celebrate, applaud and reward them when they clean their rooms, bring the car home on time, pick up the trash, and cut the grass—especially when they do it on their own volition, without threats from a dad wielding a tire tool. Imagine this dialogue:

*Why did you cut the grass, son?*
    *Because it was high. It looked as though it needed it.*
*Good! Good boy! Yes!*

Recognizing character, and admiring character, and rewarding character —that's what we have to learn. God celebrates character because character is a choice we make. Anyone can choose to have good character.

## Turn the Lights On

Leonard Ravenhill wrote, "I am not here to give a bunch of statistics that the dikes are down and this generation is about to be submerged in a hellish tide of impurities, but I am here to tell you that He that is in you is greater than he that is in the world. And the church is going to come of age in this hour. That means, as a church, as members of churches, we are not here to curse the darkness. We are here to turn on the lights. I have been in churches that condemned the darkness, but didn't do anything to turn on the lights and make life better. We, the church, are here for a purpose. We are going to turn on the lights. We are going to be relevant to the culture. We are not pathfinders. There aren't any paths to find. We have never been here before. We are pioneers, path makers blazing new trails. Look how the church has evolved thus far. Churches from past generations didn't use technology; they didn't consider having church at a different time, on a different day, for a different length of time. They lived by tradition. The church has become almost irrelevant in a rapidly changing culture with different needs. In your sphere of

> "For God, who said, 'Let there be light in the darkness,' has made us understand that this light is the brightness of the glory of God that is seen in the face of Jesus Christ"
> (2 Corinthians 4:6 NLT).

influence, I encourage you to become relevant; do not be some pious person bound by traditions that can't make a difference in the lives of those around you."

*There are hurting people everywhere—in families, schools, businesses and the church.* Answer the following questions:

- Have you allowed something or someone to convince you that you're not useful?
- Do you feel that your gifts are insufficient?
- Do you think your life will never add value to a valueless world?
- Have you bought into the lie that because of your wicked past or circumstances beyond your control, you'll never be promoted; that this is just your "lot in life?"
- Do you think God will never find you in your place of obscurity?

Here's hope from God: Stay like David on the backside of a desert, on the other side of a mountain, in a wilderness, with a right spirit, with a servant attitude—because you're a candidate for the Kingdom of the Eighth Child. God has a place for you, as he had a place for David, and God needs you.

> The church is here for a purpose. We are going to turn on the lights and be relevant to the culture.

Look at the darkness in our day. Our moral water table is dropping like a South Texas aquifer in an August drought. In a nation where Bibles are banned in schools, condoms are welcome. Jeremiah said to Israel, "You guys have forgotten how to blush," and America has lost her ability to blush as well (Jeremiah 6:15, 8:12).

I assure you that you're a candidate for the Kingdom of the Eighth Child. David was not even invited to the meeting when Samuel came to anoint a new king. But an anointing awaited him nonetheless. After seven rejects were passed before him, the prophet Samuel asked Jesse if he had any more sons. Some theologians believe that Jesse didn't invite David because he was illegitimate. That is only speculation based on circumstantial evidence. In Psalm 51:5 (KJV), David writes, *"I was shapen in iniquity, and in sin did my mother conceive me."* This biblical allusion and secular stories indicate that David possibly could have been the love child of Jesse's affair.

## God Will Wait for You

Jesse was embarrassed; he didn't count David as one of his true sons, and didn't invite him. However, while the Magnificent Seven were parading past the prophet in all their glory, so proud and handsome, God's eyes were on the backside of a desert, on the other side of a mountain, looking for the eighth child. Looking for the one nobody would pick, the least likely to succeed.

When Jesse finally mentioned David, Samuel got excited. Let's pick up the story in 1 Samuel 16:11, "We won't sit down until he gets here." Samuel said the whole program of God is standing still until that eighth child gets here. Nothing is going to move until the one who has been named gets here.

## Believe in God in Spite of the Circumstances

Who is waiting on you to move, to make yourself available? What business is waiting on you? What school is waiting on you? What church is waiting on you? What nation is waiting on you? Samuel indicated that everyone would wait until God's chosen one arrived. God might be saying to you, "*Wake up, Rumplestiltskin, God is calling you.*" Yes, God loves you. God wants to save you. God wants to use you, and you're holding back.

> Faith doesn't mean that you believe in God in spite of circumstances. Faith means you obey God in spite of consequences.

You could be the key difference in technology, education, creative thinking, arts, drama, or business.

Give yourself a chance, even if you don't believe in you, your parents don't believe in you, or your spouse doesn't believe in you. You're welcome in the Kingdom of the Eighth Child. Faith doesn't mean that you believe in God in spite of circumstances. Faith means you obey God in spite of consequences.

In Romans 8:19, Paul writes, "The creation waits in eager expectation for the sons of God to be revealed" (NIV). Paul is saying to us, "Something is going to happen that hasn't happened yet. There is coming a day when God's sons are going to come into an inheritance and all of heaven is standing on tip-toes wondering when that generation will arise."

I believe we're that generation, and God is going to visit us. The Book of Revelation is a book of symbols and sevens. In chapter 8 there are seven angels, seven trumpets, seven vials and seven churches. My paraphrase of the first three verses reads,

> *"Seven judgment angels appear to judge the earth but they are put on hold by God and another angel comes. That angel takes a censer and puts the incense in it. And God says, These are the prayers of all the saints that have ever lived and they are being poured on a generation."* So God says, *"Wait a minute, you seven angels of judgment, STOP, hold on until the eighth angel does something. And the eighth angel takes all the prayers of all the saints of all the ages and pours them out on a generation living just before judgment."*

Can you imagine the power that will come to the generation that receives the prayers of Paul, Jesus, the apostles and all the Christians that have preceded us? Things are getting worse and worse in the world, but God says we are supposed to be getting better. He promises through the Prophet Haggai that, "The glory of the last house, the church, shall exceed the glory of the former" (Haggai 2:9). That hasn't happened yet, so we have a bright future. We ought to be hopeful, optimistic and ever faithful.

> Can you imagine the power that will come to the generation that receives the prayers of Paul, Jesus, the apostles and all the Christians that have preceded us?

## Are You On Fire?

Samuel is about to give up on his mission and then David, the eighth son, shows up and God speaks, "There he is. He is the one. That's my choice." Do you feel like David must have felt before God chose him—forgotten, and overlooked by parents, school, your community, and life? Don't despair. Know that you're a candidate, like David, for the Kingdom of the Eighth Child.

Remember, God chooses from the rear of the line, and God is waiting for you. You might feel that you've been on the other side of a mountain, in a minimum wage job, unnoticed, unsolicited, and wasting your time. You're never wasting your time. Be faithful, be excellent and serve because that's what David did, and that's what other great men and women in the Bible did.

Joseph was called and anointed to be a leader, but before that, he was kidnapped and sold into slavery, abused for seventeen years and finally imprisoned. All along, he was faithful, and he served with excellence. Then God chose him as ruler of Egypt. God seems to choose that way.

The fire of God's anointing is going to fall on you. You're in the Kingdom of the Eighth Child. "Be not weary," Paul says, "in well-doing. For in due season, you will reap if you don't quit" (Galatians 6:9).

## Kingdom of the Eighth Child "Hall of Fame"

> ————◆————
>
> Moses, David, Esther, Amos, Elijah, Zacharias, Timothy, Rahab, Gideon—God chose them all for the "Kingdom of the Eighth Child." And now He wants you.
>
> ————◆————

Listen to where the great leaders in the Bible came from. They were people just like us. They were outsiders, inconspicuous outsiders. If we asked them what they were doing when God called them, what do you think their response would be?

Moses, where were you? *On the back side of a desert, running for my life. I killed an Egyptian. I had been keeping sheep for 40 years, going nowhere.*

Esther, who were you? *An orphan girl in Babylon.* She was an attractive woman leading an ordinary life. And who would have dreamed something as carnal as a beauty pageant would be the place God would pick her? God led the king of a heathen nation to notice her, and the king, not knowing she was Jewish, married her. She turned his heart to save the nation of

Israel. I wouldn't see anything inspiring in a beauty contest, but God did. God did! God is greater and wiser than your problem or sin or flesh. God can use anyone to build His kingdom.

Amos, who were you? *I was neither a prophet nor the son of a prophet. I was a farmer.*

Elijah, who were you? *I was a mountain man, a redneck hillbilly—and God chose me!*

Elijah, where did you come from? *Working the land. I was plowing, and God took me into the Kingdom of the Eighth Child.*

Zacchaeus, who were you? *I was a tax collector—an IRS Agent—ripping off my own Jewish people for the Roman government. I had an inferiority complex because I was short. I was up a tree when Jesus chose me.* Up a tree when Jesus chose him!

Timothy, who were you? *Well, my father was half-Greek, my mother was Jewish—I was not even supposed to be in this thing called a church. I was a half-breed.*

Rahab, who were you? *A high-priced, tax-paying prostitute working the high rent district of Jericho, catering to the needs of the city fathers.* And God chose her!

Gideon, who were you? *I was a coward, hiding in a wine-press and God showed up and said, "You are a mighty man of valor. You are going to deliver my people." Me? I am on the back side of a mountain. I am the least likely to succeed. And God said something like, "Good, you're going to be in the Kingdom of the Eighth Child. You're the one I will use."*

All the great leaders of the Bible came from the Kingdom of the Eighth Child.

## God Will Stop for You

God wants to do something with you, and He will hold up His program until you show up. He stopped the sun for Joshua (Joshua 10:12-13). He backed it up ten degrees. He made Sarah's womb fertile when she was 90 years old (Genesis 21:1-2). He stopped the flow of the Jordan River for the Ark of the Covenant (Joshua 3:13). He split the Red Sea for Moses and the Children of Israel (Exodus 14:21). When He chooses you, everything goes on hold until you show up.

Why was David chosen? One day, a lion jumped his daddy's flock of sheep. David, did you ever read a manual? Did you listen to any tapes on lion killing? Listen to how David might have replied,

> *"No, I never even went to seminary. But there was a need. I didn't have time to think about manuals, ordination papers, or anything else. There was a need. I was available. I just grabbed hold of the lion and suddenly I found strength I didn't know I had. Same story with a bear. I am just a shepherd boy. I play a little guitar, write a few songs. I haven't sold anything but I am available."*

One day, a giant comes around. David could have said,

> *"I never read up on giant killing either. I wasn't wearing any armor, but I remembered the lion and the bear and I remembered the*

> *anointing that came on me when there was a job to be done. So suddenly the giant came, and I said, 'Who is this uncircumcised Philistine that he should defy the armies of God?' I can't explain what happened."*

And that is the principle of the Kingdom of the Eighth Child. The eighth child is God's choice, often the last person in the line, but one who makes himself or herself available.

David wasn't intimidated, and you shouldn't be either. You shouldn't be intimidated by others' successes. If you've made mistakes, broken laws, disappointed your family, or felt like a fool, that's not the end of your story. Maybe your parents or your peers shunned you, and now you've set your expectations low. Don't despair. Don't cling to the past. God knows where you are, and He needs you.

David's wife, Bathsheba, was an adulteress, but God found her and made her the mother of Solomon, the greatest king in the nation of Israel.

Listen to what I am saying: *This is our day.* This is the day God chooses nobodies. This is the day God chooses the weak. This is our day, the day for the little guy, the nobody, the unqualified and the contemptible. Don't you see the pattern? God resists the proud . . . but He gives grace to the humble. This isn't to say that God

> "God resists the proud, but gives grace to the humble"
> (James 4:6 NKJV).

approves of the actions of the adulteress or the thief.

They will be judged, of course. But there is hope for them in God's eyes. God only resists the proud.

We all want the anointing. We all want to be successful. We all want to prosper. But some in the Bible did not survive their anointing. Lucifer was the anointed cherub who covered the throne of God . . . but his anointing made him proud. He said, "*I will be like the Most High.*" He led the first rebellion in heaven and took a third of the angels with him . . . and God cast them down to the earth. We could learn from this. When you get into pride, Satan gets the day off. He doesn't have to fight you any more: God will resist you (read James 4:6, 1 Peter 5:5).

Most of the eighth child members came from such abominable lifestyles and pitiful pasts of sin, tragedy, inferiority, insecurity or failure that not one of them had pride. It was by the grace of God that He would use them at all. They had low self-esteem and thought they weren't worthy, and they were grateful for the grace of God.

We've all seen what can happen when a talented person suddenly finds success. That person can become arrogant, patronizing. He can preach down to you, and that's despicable and demeaning. When I'm down, the last thing I need is somebody slapping me down. I need somebody to say there's hope.

> Quit slapping people down. Offer them hope.

The Bible says, "*The word of the Lord came to Jonah a second time*" (Jonah 3:1). He was foolish and didn't obey the first time. Some of us are second, third and seventeenth repeat offenders. Thank God, He is the God of second chances or third chances or twentieth chances. He doesn't choose from the front of the line. He chooses all the way back at the end of the line, a position in life with which you might be familiar.

When David fled from Saul, he lived in a cave. He lived off the land. He served as a mercenary, was a nuisance to the system. He was a political outsider. You might be just that way, for right now. But your day is coming. Just like David—an outsider chosen by God to become an insider. David was selected from the nobodies below to the hierarchy above and became king of Israel. God said of David, "*He has a heart after my heart*" (1 Samuel 13:14). He wasn't a perfect man. He had a great heart filled with humility.

## Make Yourself Available

Thank God for grace. God is always looking to the back of the line. The kingdom of God was intended to be given, not inherited, and it wasn't given to people who played their spiritual cards right. It was given to those who wanted the anointing, who wanted God to use them. They were available from the least to the eighth child. If today you're intimidated, God wants you to make yourself available.

Present yourself to the Lord. If you go through the Bible, you'll find many instances where people presented themselves to the Lord. You might say,

> *"I don't know what God wants me to do. I don't know if He could do anything with me, but I love Him and I am going to present myself to Him and say, Here am I. Send me. I am available."*

> The kingdom of God is given to those who want the anointing, who want God to use them.

That's all you can be—available. And wherever you find yourself today, just be faithful.

Darlene Zschech, one of the leading praise and worship leaders in the world, was in the back of the line and standing in the back of the choir at Hillsong Church in Sidney, Australia. She was licking stamps in the mailroom. She didn't have any albums. And God reached in the back of the line and picked out somebody who wasn't ambitious, somebody who was just faithful and who said, "I am available."

God brought her to the front. I was there with Brian Houston, Senior Pastor of Hillsong Church, on the front row, when Darlene and the Hillsong team sang for the very first time, "Shout to the Lord." It was their first praise song that would be heard around the world . . . and the rest is history.

God resists the proud. That's why we don't beat people up in the church that I pastor. We lift them up and encourage them. We might beat up on the proud, but we don't beat up those who have fallen, who feel like nothing. We aren't after you. We're after the proud, contemptible Pharisee, the self-righteous bigot who will harm you at the drop of a hat and bite faster than a Texas rattlesnake.

In my ministry, it's my wish to be a help and a blessing to people. Not long ago, a wife brought her husband to my church for their anniversary. He had said, "Honey, I'll give you anything you want for our 25th wedding anniversary."

She said, "I want you to go to church with me." He hadn't been in church in twenty-five years. He didn't want to, but he said, "I told you I would do anything you wanted so I will go."

Since that anniversary day, he has faithfully brought his wife to church. After his first time with us, he said, "I had never heard a message like that." He felt hopeful; he felt included. He didn't feel preached down to. He believed in the possibility that God could use him, forgive him, and love him.

I invite you, too, to know that wherever you have been, God welcomes you back. You're invited to *the Kingdom of the Eighth Child.*

In 1 Corinthians 1:26-31, Paul's words say it all: "Remember, dear brothers and sisters, that few of you were wise in the world's eyes or powerful or wealthy when God called you. Instead, God deliberately chose things the world considers foolish in order to shame those who think they are wise. And He chooses those who are powerless to shame those who are powerful. God chose things despised by the world, things counted as nothing at all, and used them to bring to nothing what the world considers important so that no one can boast in the presence of God. God alone made it possible for you to be in Christ Jesus. For our benefit, God made Christ to be wisdom. He, Christ, is the one who made us acceptable to God. He made us pure and holy. He gave himself to purchase our freedom" (NLT).

> —— • ◆ • ——
>
> "God chose things the world considers foolish to shame those who think they are wise . . . those who are powerless to shame those who are powerful . . . things despised by the world, things counted as nothing at all . . . to bring to nothing what the world considers important so that no one can boast in the presence of God"
> (1 Corinthians 1:27 NLT).
>
> —— • ◆ • ——

As Scripture says, the person who wishes to boast or brag should boast only of what the Lord has done. That's why God chooses the weak, the lowly, the one at the back of the line—so nobody can boast except to say, "Look what the Lord has done."

## Come Out of Obscurity

I never will forget a time years ago when I was preaching in Tulsa to about 18,000 people and I talked about A-level Christianity. Unknown to me, there was a man among us that day who had been ministering with 400 impoverished people in West Virginia, dealing with horrific poverty. This man had no influence, no magnitude and no name. He was sitting behind me with a group of preachers. You probably know him. He was T.D. Jakes—at that time, he was unnoticed and undiscovered.

Then one day, God chose this nobody from West Virginia. Who? T.D. Jakes? But no one knew him except the 400 folks he was serving in God's name. Yet God saw something in him, like David. God is gracious and took that hardworking man out of obscurity. He brought him to Dallas, Texas, and gave him a pulpit that has drawn masses.

Today T.D. Jakes is an anomaly, a phenomenon. That potential was hidden away in rural West Virginia, but he was faithful and God chose from the back of the line. Bishops and big boys were running around with their big rings and entourages, puffed up with their importance. Then this unknown preacher from West Virginia showed up. And the proud dropped aside like the seven sons of Jesse because God chose him.

> We are heirs to the past, guardians of the present, and architects of the future.

Are you like T.D. Jakes? God might choose you to do something that will change the world. Regardless of your past, God is going to cleanse you. You might produce a child who will change the world, as Bathsheba did.

God is always looking at the heart. We don't know what is in the heart of somebody involved in a bad business, a scam, a criminal act. They might be ignorant. They might not know the grace of God or they might have been exposed to too much religious pride. We don't know, but God knows. And when God speaks to someone who has strayed, He can melt a heart, and bring forth tears and ultimately the miracle of change. God can do anything.

One of the musicians in my church is a phenomenal guitar player. He had been playing at a nightclub and he gave his life to Jesus. One night, playing for some swingers at the nightclub, he prayed, "*Lord, please use me. Is there anything you need me to do?*"

He was coming to my church, but I didn't know who he was, but God knew. This young man looked in the bulletin and saw a notice that musicians were needed for the church band. The rest is history. These days, he plays for my church, he's still swinging, but with a different partner—as a gifted member of our band.

John the Baptist came on the scene and no one knew him, either. He didn't have a public relations department. He started his church in a bad location—the wilderness. He didn't have style. He wore camel hair clothes. He didn't have a dark power suit. His diet of locusts and wild honey left something to be desired. The only thing John had going for him was that he was anointed. And people left the city to walk all the way out in the country to hear him speak. They must have passed 100 synagogues, but they came. John was in the Kingdom of the Eighth Child.

Here is the good news: Today, you might be in an obscure place. You might be in a third world country. It doesn't matter. God can reach anywhere. He has reached into Ghana; He has reached into Kenya; He has reached into Johannesburg, South Africa. He has reached all over the world in the most obscure places for people who were available. It doesn't matter.

Maybe you're in a job or a career where you feel unnoticed, unappreciated. Maybe you just blend into the background. You might be asking, "Does anybody notice me?" Yes, God is always looking on the backside of the wilderness. There is Moses keeping sheep—40 years alone. There is David—unchosen, a nobody. God had His eye on David, though. There is Esther—a beautiful little orphan girl, just a refugee in Babylon, but God says,

"*I birthed her that way because I have a plan for her.*" And in spite of her lowly station in life, everything in the nation and everything in the New Testament hinged on her. And she responds. In fact, without her, Babylon would have killed all the Jews, and we wouldn't have Jesus today. You might need to rethink your paradigm. I am.

> Make yourself available to God and He will search for you in the most obscure place.

If you're a parent, don't worry about what God can do with your kids. Maybe you can't handle them, maybe the schoolteachers can't handle them, maybe nobody right now can handle them—God can handle them. Pray for their hearts. I pray for my children to have pure and tender hearts. I tell you one thing—my own exterior can seem pretty hard sometimes, but God always knows that my heart is tender.

And that's why God can use people the rest of us might ignore and why He will save people you might not expect. And promote people you would never pick. He can read our hearts.

This is your day. Whether you're young or not so young, God has a future for you. Maybe your parents tossed you out, gave up on you. Maybe you even deserved it. But God didn't throw you away.

God will pick the least likely. Not those in the front, but those in the back—the weak, the obscure, those who might have gone unnoticed by ordinary people. He will wait for you.

In hiding? Come out. God is bringing you from the end of the line to the front. Your potential is before you. You thought you were empty, but God sees you full of grace, potential and promise. Come out! You belong to the *Kingdom of the Eighth Child.*

## Amazing Keys to Your Potential

1. God chooses nobodies. You can be the "nobody" whom God chooses to do great things.

2. God is looking for people who choose character over appearance or charisma.

3. Make yourself available. God wants to use you.

4. If you're in an obscure place, get ready! God sees your potential and is about to move you from the end of the line to the front!

# Get On With It— Live Full!

I n this last word, I simply want to reiterate and remind you of these keys to your potential in God:

You're a unique specimen. There will never be another you. When you introduce yourself, ecstatically proclaim, "Hello, meet an original!"

Jesus didn't die to make you valuable. He died to prove how valuable, how precious you are to Him. Your personal price tag is amazing—you're worth the death of the Son of God. On your worst day, you are worth the death of Jesus.

What a valuable person you are! Never demean yourself. When you look in the mirror, say,

*"I am a person of heavenly value.*
*God did a good thing when He made me!"*

No matter how wretched you've been, no matter how unimportant you might feel—if you're still alive and breathing, there's something that God still wants you to do.

Try to imagine God with all possibility inside Him, before anything was. You couldn't recognize the infinite possibilities because all things would still be in the form of potential.

Remember that . . .

- You have a future.
- You have a treasure inside you.
- You're illuminated with the supernatural power of God's Holy Spirit.
- God's message to you is, "I love you; you're valuable."
- The Holy Spirit's power is in you and gives you the power to change.

In the days ahead, pay close attention to the extraordinary potential of the ordinary. If you're faithful, if you pray and listen to God, then what He speaks to you will come to pass right where you are.

**Never underestimate the power of a personal word from God to you. When God speaks a word to you, you will feel His life, energy and power.**

Never hesitate to say *Yes!* to any offer God makes you. God has already made a way for you. It's your job to say, "Where You lead, I will follow."

## 7 Keys of Purpose for Your Life

1. God's purpose for you preceded His creation of you.

2. Your purpose determines your design.

3. Your purpose predicts your potential.

4. God's purpose is nestled neatly in your nature.

5. Your purpose and calling coincide with your gifts and abilities.

6. God provides for His purpose, not your plans.

7. Learn to soar with your strengths and manage your weaknesses.

God will make you prosperous, productive and fruitful in the land of your affliction. Don't get stuck in self-pity! When you're knocked down; get up, dust yourself off, and be productive. Stop praying and whining, "Oh, God, why did this happen to me?" Start doing and God will bless you! Your obstacle or problem is your gateway to significance and promotion. God can turn your disappointment into His divine appointment.

You might feel insignificant, but remember that God chooses nobodies. You can be the nobody God chooses to do great things. God is looking for people like you who choose character over appearance, charisma or talent. Make yourself available. God wants to use you.

If you're in an obscure place, get ready! God sees your potential and is about to move you from the end of the line to the front!

Now go for it. *Live life full, and when you die, die empty!*

# Other Books by Rick Godwin

### *Training for Reigning*

If you want to stay in mediocrity and powerless ritual, don't read this book! You will be greatly challenged by these scriptural insights to grow into a real spiritual lifestyle that Jesus taught for all His disciples. Rick brings tremendous conviction, but also tremendous encouragement to be all God has called us to be.

### *Exposing Witchcraft in the Church*

"Rick Godwin is anointed of the Lord to shake us out of our religious traditions and bring the power of the Word back in to focus."

—Casey Treat, Pastor
Christian Faith Center,
Seattle, Washington

### *Flying Higher: Seven Keys to Making Godly Choices*

Stop struggling alone to know God's will for your next decision, God's timing for your next answer to prayer or God's way to solve your problem.

Just as an experienced pilot knows how to use his airplane's navigational guidance system no matter what the conditions, you'll learn how to rise above the confusion that has grounded many along life's journey. No more living by sight alone; you're on your way to flying higher with God.

# Contact Information

For additional information on audio and video resources by Rick Godwin, please contact:

## Rick Godwin Ministries
ATTN: Bookstore
14015 San Pedro Ave.
San Antonio, TX 78232-4337
Tel: 800-675-3297
Tel: 210-491-4484